Maine Island Classics

Living and Knitting on a Maine Island

North Island Designs

Maine Island Classics

Living and Knitting on a Maine Island

by Chellie Pingree and Debby Anderson
Photos by Peter Ralston

20 KNITTING PATTERNS FROM
NORTH ISLAND DESIGNS

Down East Books
Camden, Maine

ISBN 0-89272-315-7

Photography by Peter Ralston
Design and production by Michael Mahan Graphics
Typeset by Black Spruce Type/Graphics

Printed and bound in Hong Kong through Four Colour Imports

10   9   8   7   6   5   4

Down East Books, Camden, Maine

Table of Contents

Maine Island Classics

A rugged coastline, blue green spruce, fields of wild flowers dotted with grazing sheep, sailboats crossing the bay; such images of island life are reflected in the sweaters of North Island Designs. These contemporary designs leave you with the feeling of a classic sweater—one that you may pass on for generations.

The patterns in this book are the work of Debby Anderson, with the Maine islands as her primary source of inspiration—the changing seasons, the diversity of life and the great beauty of the surroundings. Design is around us everywhere: lobster traps resting in the winter snow, a sailboat silhouetted in a sunset, wild asters with a backdrop of a stone wall, the subtle colors and the arrangement of natural objects give inspiration for what is produced in these patterns.

North Island Designs has been in business for three years, the offspring of a retail store owned by Chellie Pingree coupled with the design ideas of Debby. In this time the company has sold thousands of kits through catalogues and over 1000 retail stores throughout the country. Although the company continues to produce new kits every season we have decided to answer our customers' requests and print some favorites in this pattern book.

Several employees assist in the production of kits and have been invaluable in the production of this book. Some are islanders whose families have lived here for many generations, others are "transplants," the local term for residents who are originally from away (it takes several generations to lose this status). They climb the stairs to our second story production area to run the machines that wind yarn for our kits, answer the phone, pack and ship, as well as drink a little coffee and share a few stories. Without them North Island Designs wouldn't be a business and this book wouldn't be a reality. We thank them and the many members of the community who have offered their support and frequent words of advice.

We hope you will enjoy these patterns and continue to knit classics for your friends, your family and yourself.

Before You Begin Knitting These Patterns...

A few words on knitting and technique from Debby:

Most of us don't have to make our own clothes anymore, and it isn't usually any cheaper, so I wonder, why do I bother to knit? I've decided I do it because it is good for my soul. Somehow when my fingers are occupied creating something beautiful and warm, my mind is free to ponder and grow. Most of our time today is so crowded with activities and obligations, it's hard to find a moment for just thinking. Knitting allows you to do both with the added bonus of a homemade treasure.

Gauge

Before you start any project, check your gauge. All sweaters are designed to be knit with a certain number of stitches to the inch and this is far more important than the suggested needle size. The most important step is that you choose the size of needles that will allow you to achieve the required number of stitches to the inch.

To do this, knit a small swatch about 20 stitches wide by three inches high using the main color and the larger of the suggested needles. When you are done, gently press with a damp cloth, then let it cool. Now, measure two inches across and count the stitches; divide this number by two and you've got your gauge. If you have fewer stitches per inch than the gauge given in the pattern, decrease the size of your needles; if too many, increase the size of your needles, and knit a swatch again. This step is very important to achieve the garment you want, no matter how many years you have been knitting.

Ribbing

When you are casting on the lower edge, remember that the ribbing is intended to be elastic as the garment is worn. If you have a tendency to cast on too tightly, use a larger needle to cast on the stitches. Also remember to bind off neck stitches loosely so that the ribbing can stretch to go over your head.

When a pattern calls for K1, P1 ribbing it is hard to go wrong. However, you will notice that in some of my patterns I have used a K2, P1 ribbing. When my sister-in-law was just learning to knit, she very ambitiously started the chicken sweater. The next time she came to visit she proudly showed me the front and I noticed she had done exactly what I said—K2, P1, but on both sides! It produced a very unique look, to say the least, but it will not have the stretch of ribbing done the correct way. To avoid having her start over I suggested she duplicate it on the back and cuffs. The lesson here is—work your ribbing K2, P1 on the right side and K1, P2 when you turn the piece over.

Multi-Color Knitting

Knitting with two or more colors is very easy and if you have never done it before, now is a perfect time to start!! Knit a small swatch to practice and you will be surprised how simple it is.

When I am knitting with two colors, I don't tie a new color on until I have knit a few stitches with it—I then go back and make a simple small knot. If you can weave the end in without making a knot at all, it is better, but I find that if I don't attach it somehow, the stitches will have a tendency to loosen up. When you are carrying colors, it is important to only carry the unused color for no more than three or four stitches before twisting the yarns together. If you don't you will end up with a long piece on the inside where its easy to get your fingers caught when you are putting on the sweater.

I like to use bobbins and short pieces of yarn and even attach new balls of the background color rather than carry the colors behind. This way the design will not pucker. You are left with a lot of ends to weave in, but try to relax and enjoy it—a nice sweater takes time to complete.

Mistakes in two color knitting can be corrected by duplicate stitch (see page 9) after the garment is complete. (We also often use duplicate stitch in areas where only a small amount of color is called for.) A color out of place here or there won't make a great difference. As my mother used to say "It will never be noticed on a galloping horse!"

Putting Your Sweater Together

When all of the pieces have been finished, I think it is very important to press (block) them before sewing together. To sew the seams, I put the right sides together, take a straight needle (about a number 5) and use it as a large pin to hold the pieces while I sew them together using a back stitch. I sew the shoulders first (unless the pattern has called for knitting them together), then the neck ribbing, the side seams and sleeve seams. Last of all I turn the body wrong side out and insert the sleeve so that the right sides are together. Match the seams at the underarms and shoulders. Ease the sleeve cap to fit and sew using a back stitch. Press all of your seams.

Choosing a Size

Figuring out what size to make is a very logical process. Begin by finding a sweater that fits the way you (or your sweater recipient) really like a sweater to fit. Then, measure across the chest, the sleeve length, the length of the sweater, etc. Here is where the stitch gauge becomes important again. If you want your sweater to measure 40″ across the chest and there are 4 stitches per inch with the type of yarn you are using, you will need approximately 80 stitches on the front and back along with a couple of extra stitches for the seams. In our patterns, the measurements represent actual sweater measurements, not chest size of the wearer.

Pattern Variations

You will find that some of the patterns in this book are printed with more than one choice of gauge which gives you the option of knitting in several different kinds of yarn. There are also cardigan variations for several of the patterns—select the style which works best for you.

Embroidery

A few embroidery stitches can be a great addition to a sweater—a spark of color as well as texture, a way to make a garment unique. Here is an explanation of the simple stitches we have included in some of the patterns in this book.

French Knot

This is the perfect stitch for little round things like apples or flowers in a field. Bring the yarn up through the sweater where you want the knot to be and wind the yarn around the needle 3 to 5 times close to the sweater. Then insert the needle close by and hold the twisted yarn with your thumb while you pull the needle gently all the way through to form a knot.

Outline Stitch

This is somewhat like a back stitch except that each stitch is started just beside and behind the end of the previous stitch, creating a heavier line.

Loop Stitch

Bring the yarn up through the sweater to form a loop and insert the needle close to the same spot. Then bring the needle back up to catch the other end of the loop.

Duplicate Stitch

Use this stitch to correct a mistake or to add a stitch in another color after the sweater is complete. Pull the needle up through the stitch below the one to be covered. Pass the needle under both sides of the stitch above the one to be covered and back down through the stitch where the yarn entered.

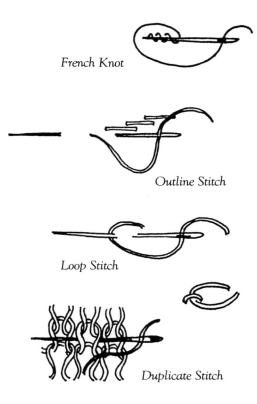

French Knot

Outline Stitch

Loop Stitch

Duplicate Stitch

Glossary of Terms

st, sts	stitch, stitches
k	knit
p	purl
st st	stockinette stitch
incr	increase
bet	between
dec	decrease
rnd	round
rem	remaining
oz	ounce
tog	together
k 2 tog	knit two stitches together
in	inch
approx	approximately
beg	beginning
MC	main color

10

Islands as a Source of Design

Of all of the unusual characteristics of life on an island which get discussed—the social structures, the complicated logistics, the economic difficulties—it is easy to forget the role that its remarkable beauty plays in our lives. Most striking is the lack of development and the attendant insults to the eye that an overabundance of man-made objects creates. There are no fast food restaurants, discount stores covering large acreages or even much trash along the sides of the roads. This environment allows an abundance of design possibilities and a peaceful setting to work in with fewer of the complications which usually serve as sidetracks.

Without the distractions, we are left with colors, patterns, shapes—designs that become a part of everyone's life. In spring, the subtle blends of the tree colors, predominantly rich green spruce with an occasional dark red swamp maple and the new buds of bright green birches, stand out behind the old fields. The fields are golden-brown, with the spring green young growth beginning to emerge, and framed with moss covered gray stone walls.

Every season lends a different feeling: the bright colored wild flowers of summer— purple lupines, white daisies, red and orange Indian paintbrush dotting the green fields; sailboats crossing the bay, lobster traps and buoys piled on the weathered wooden and granite wharves awaiting transport to the fishing grounds; peach and lilac sunsets, with the rolling patterns of hills and the many colors of water in the foreground.

There are also the whimsical and humorous parts of the natural world to be observed and incorporated. Chickens scratch the ground endlessly in search of edible treasures. In groups they set up pecking order societies, chasing each other for infractions of the rules and communicating endlessly in a language of low guttural sounds, punctuated with high shrieks and cackles. Sheep with their timidity; cats, both tame and wild with their playfulness; even sea life, the weather and the tides all create feelings and ideas that somehow get translated into the colors and patterns that make up our designs. Islands have proved to be a generous resource from which to draw.

Debby's Design Technique

Debby has been knitting since she was 10 and has been creating patterns for many years. When she was primarily a home-maker she made creative and original pre-sents for everyone and translated these talents into a business when she opened her doll shop in 1978 and sold her original molded felt dolls there. She also designed a line of patterns for the popular Sasha doll (sadly, the doll has now been discontinued) including many miniature sweaters. Creating is in her blood; Debby's mother is an accom-plished water color artist and Debby studies painting, drawing and sculpture in her spare time.

Asked where her design inspirations come from, Debby would reply "Island life" and asked again "Where?", she would say, "In the bathtub." Debby lives in a small house at the base of the road that leads to the nine house neighborhood known as Sleepyville.

Their house was built in the early 1900's by a summer family as a house for the captain of their boat but has long been in use as a year round home. Few structural changes have been made since then and the original claw footed bathtub is where the Anderson family gets clean and where Debby spends some time each morning thinking things over and plotting her day. Hence, from there she has made many quick exits to paper and pencil as a design came to her.

To create a pattern, Debby first graphs her inspiration on paper and then with a box of many colored yarns in front of her, chooses the colors. She then knits the design, making modifications to the graph and colors as the pattern reveals itself. Before finalizing a pattern, she will often knit the garment a second time, usually finding shortcuts and making useful changes.

Sophisticated Chickens

Hens have always seemed very comical to me and in this sweater I have coupled the scratching hens, modeled after the ones I keep behind the house, with the pattern from the chicken wire fence. I have always been fascinated by the way chicken wire is put together, with the wire for each hole making up part of the next one. To replicate the design on this sweater I purl on the right side and knit on the wrong side—the effect is most noticeable in the lighter colors.

The kernels of corn can be done in duplicate stitch or french knots after completion. The chicken legs should be done in a dark yarn if you are using a light background, and in yellow if your background is dark.

Needles: US 5 and 9—or whatever size needed to get a stitch gauge of 4 sts = 1 in. using Knitting Worsted Yarn
Sizes: 38 (40,42)
Materials:
5 (4oz) skeins Main Color
10 yds each White and Brown Tweed for Chickens
5 yds each Red, Yellow and Dark Sheeps Gray

Front

Using larger needle, cast on 72 (78,81) sts. Change to smaller needles and work K2, P1, ribbing for 4 inches, increasing 7 (5,6) sts evenly across in last row of ribbing. Change to larger needles and follow chart for front panel . Work till 13½ (14,14) inches or desired length to underarm. End on right side. With wrong side facing you, knit next three rows to form 2 ridges on right side of work. *Armholes:* Bind off 5 sts beg next two rows, also work design. Decrease 1 st each end every other row 5 times.

At neck, work 20 (22,24) sts. Place remaining sts on holder. Dec 1 st every other row at neck edge 4 times. Bind off 5(6,7) sts at shoulder edge 2 times, then 6(6,6) sts. Leave 19 center sts on holder; work remaining 20 (22,24) sts to correspond.

Back

Cast on 72 (78,81) sts. Work same as front until 14(14½, 14½) inches or desired length. Continue panel of chicken wire all the way up back and do armholes same as front. Work shoulders and place 27 sts of neck on holder.

Sleeves

Cast on 39 (42,42) sts. Rib in K2, P1 for 3 inches. Increase 4 (3,5) sts last row of ribbing. Change to larger needles and follow chart for panel. Knit 8 (9,10) sts, work 27 sts for panel, knit 8 (9,10) sts. Increase 1 st each side every 8th row 7 times. Work on 57 (59,61) sts till 16 (16½,17) inches or desired length to underarm. Bind off 5 sts beg next 2 rows. Dec 1 st each end every other row same as armhole till 24 sts remain. Bind off 3 sts beg next 4 rows. Bind off remaining sts.

Finishing

Sew left shoulder seam. Pick up and knit sts on holders and 12 (12,14) sts at each neck edge. Work ribbing of K2, P1 for 1 inch. Bind off very loosely using larger needles. Sew seams, and weave ends in.

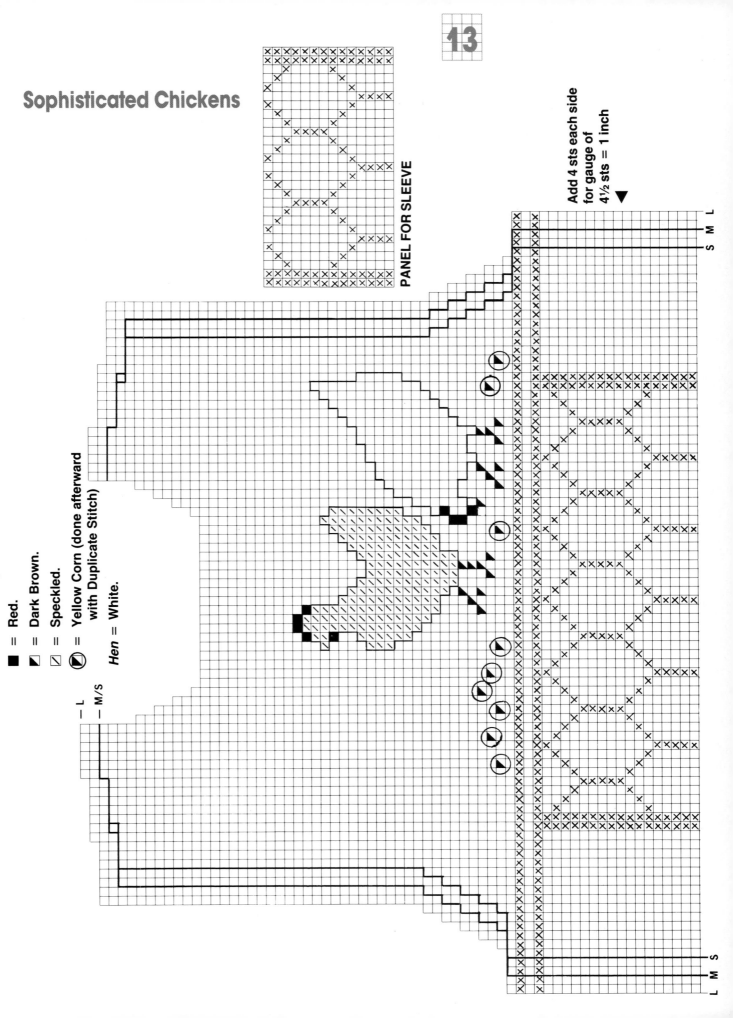

Sophisticated Chickens

PANEL FOR SLEEVE

Add 4 sts each side
for gauge of
4½ sts = 1 inch ▼

⊠ = Knit on purl side, or vice versa.

■ = Red.

◣ = Dark Brown.

◺ = Speckled.

⦸ = Yellow Corn (done afterward
with Duplicate Stitch)

Hen = White.

Sophisticated Chickens Pullover

Chicken Cardigan

Chicken Cardigan

Sizes: 38 (40,42)
Needles: US 5 and 9—or whatever size needed to get a stitch gauge of 4 sts = 1 in. using Knitting Worsted Yarn
Materials:
5 (4oz) skeins Main Color
10 yds each White and Brown Tweed for Chickens
5 yds each Red, Yellow and Dark Sheeps Gray
Buttons: 6 Pewter Buttons

Back

With smaller needles, cast on 72 (78,81) sts. Work K2, P1 ribbing for 4 inches, increasing 7 (5,6) sts evenly across row—79 (83,87) sts. Change to larger needles and follow chart for back panel. Work till 13½ (14,14½) inches or desired length to underarm. *Armhole:* Bind off 5 sts beginning next 2 rows, then dec 1 st each end every other row 5 times. Work 31 (31,33) more rows. Bind off 5 (6,7) sts at shoulder edge beg next 4 rows, then 6 sts beg next 2 rows. Place center 27 sts on holder.

Left Front

With smaller needles, cast on 41 (44,47) sts. Work K2, P1 ribbing on first 36 (39,42) sts, then seed-stitch (K1,P1,K1,P1,K1) on remaining 5 sts. Next row: K1,P1,K1,P1,K1 first 5 sts, then K1,P2 across row. Continue in ribbing for 4 inches, increasing 3 (2,1) sts evenly across last row of ribbing. Change to larger needles, and work stockinette st first 13 (15,17) sts. Then follow chart for chicken-wire pattern. Work armholes same as back. Work neck as follows: Place 14 sts on holder, then dec 1 st at neck edge every other row 4 times. Decrease shoulder to correspond to back.

Right Front

Work same as left front, only a mirror image, and work 6 buttonholes evenly spaced on button band. To work buttonhole: work to within 4 sts of end of row, bind off 2 sts firmly, finish row. Next row, cast on 2 sts over bound-off sts to make buttonhole. First buttonhole should be halfway up ribbing; last buttonhole, midway in neck ribbing; and the other four evenly spaced between.

Sleeves

Cast on 39 (42,42) sts. Rib in K2, P1 for 3 inches. Increase 4 (3,5) sts last row of ribbing. Change to larger needles and follow chart for panel. Knit (8,9,10) sts, work 27 sts for panel, knit 8 (9,10) sts. Increase 1 st each side every 8th row 7 times. Work on 57 (59,61) sts till 16(16½, 17) inches or desired length to underarm. Bind off 5 sts beg next 2 rows. Decrease 1 st each end every other row same as armhole till 24 sts remain. Bind off 3 sts beg next 4 rows. Bind off remaining sts.

Finishing

Sew shoulder seams. Using smaller needles, pick up and knit *approx* 78 sts around neck. Work seed-stitch on 5 sts each end, K2,P1 ribbing in between for 1 inch. Don't forget last buttonhole. Bind off loosely.

Sew seams, weave in loose ends. Sew on buttons.

Chicken Cardigan

☑ = Speckled.

■ = Red.

◤ = Yellow.

Hen = White.

⊠ = Knit on purl side,
or vice versa.

Chart for Left Front

S M L

Chart for Back

S M L

L M S

Chart for Sleeve

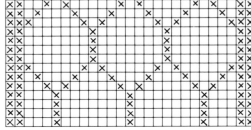

Sheep in the Meadow Cardigan

Sheep in the Meadow Pullover

Sheep in the Meadow Pullover

Materials (Pattern page 21):
Wool Knitting Worsted, 4 sts = 1 in.
5 (4 oz) skeins of the Main Color
20 Yds. White or Medium Gray (depending on whether you have chosen a light or dark background)
20 Yds. Dark Sheeps Gray

Materials (Pattern page 64):
Cotton or Cotton/Wool, 4½ sts = 1 in. Even though Cotton doesn't seem appropriate for a sheep sweater, you will find that the graph for this pattern works well with the Cable Pullover pattern on page 64 with a stitch gauge of 4½ sts to the inch, a good gauge for many of the cottons or cotton wool blends on the market. You will need:
1200 Yds. of the Main Color
20 Yds. White or Gray
20 Yds. Brown

⊙ = White or Gray.
■ = Dark.
☒ = Knit on purl side, or vice versa.

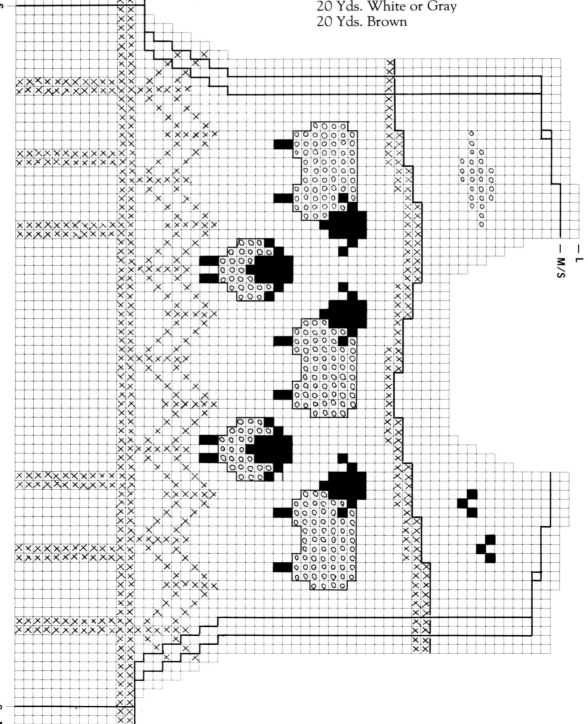

Add 4 sts each side for gauge of 4½ sts = 1 inch ▶

Versatile Cable Pullover

This is our standard cable sweater design which will be used for three of the patterns in the book—Sheep in the Meadow, Sailboat, and Appletree Sweater. It is relatively simple to knit with the cables below the yoke giving the sweater style and a good fit.

Needles: US 5 and 9—or whatever size needed to get stitch gauge of 4 sts = 1 in. *Sizes:* 36 (38,40)

Front

With #5 needles, cast on 72 (75,81) sts. Work K2,P1 ribbing for 3¼ inches, increasing 6 (7,5) sts evenly in last row, 78 (82,86). Change to #9 needles and proceed as follows:

Row 1: K8(10,12),P2,K6,P2,K6,P2,K26, P2,K6,P2,K6,P2,K8(10,12).

Row 2: P8(10,12),K2,P6,K2,P6,K2,P26, K2,P6,K2,P6,K2,P8(10,12).

Rows 3,5: Same as 1.

Rows 4,6: Same as 2.

Row 7: K8(10,12),P2,C6b (do this cable by slipping 3 sts to holder, hold in *back* of work, K3,K3 from holder), P2,C6b,P2,K26, P2,C6f (slip 3 sts to holder, hold in *front* of work, K3,K3 from holder), P2,C6f,P2, K8 (10,12).

Rows 8,10,12,14: Same as 2.

Rows 9,11,13: Same as 1.

Row 15: Repeat row 7.

Continue knitting the K sts, and purling the P ones as established, with no more cabling until work measures 11½(12,12) inches. This is the measurement that will determine length of sweater. Finished sweater length is 14(14½,14½) inches. Any adjustments should be done now. Repeat rows 7-15, then rows 2 and 3 once.

With wrong side facing you, *knit* the next three rows to make 2 ridges on the right side of work. *Start Chart (p. 20, p. 24. p. 28 or p. 65).* Armholes: Bind off 5 sts at beg of next 2 rows, 68(72,76) sts. Dec 1 st each end every other row 5 times, 58(62,66) sts. Continue following chart, row for row, until neck opening is reached. On right side, work 20(22,24) sts, placing remaining sts on holder. Dec 1 st every other row at neck edge 4 times, 16(18,20) sts. Bind off 5(6,7) sts at shoulder edge 2 times; bind off remaining 6 sts. Leave center 18 sts on holder, and work other side to correspond.

Back

Work as for front for all shapings *except neck.* Do not follow charted design on back; rather, work stockinette sts above ridges. Work shoulders, leaving center 26 sts on holder.

Sleeves

With #5 needles, cast on 39(39,42) sts. Work K2,P1 ribbing for 3 inches, increasing 3(5,4) sts in last row, 42(44,46) sts. Change to #9 needles, and establish sleeve cable as follows:

Row 1: K12(13,14),P2,K6,P2,K6,P2,K12 (13,14). Continue working the cables as for front, while increasing 1 st each side every 8th row 7 times, 56(58,60) sts. Work until sleeve measures 14½ inches. This measurement is for a 17-inch sleeve length. Any adjustments should be made now. Twist cables again (pattern rows 7-15). Work pattern rows 2,3 once. With wrong side facing, knit next 3 rows. *Sleeve Cap:* Bind off 5 sts at beg of next 2 rows. Dec 1 st at beg of every row in same manner as for armhole, until 24 sts remain. Bind off 3 sts at beg of next 4 rows; bind off remaining sts.

Finishing

Sew left shoulder seam. Pick up approximately 72 sts, and work in K2,P1 for 1 inch. Bind off loosely in ribbing using #9 needles. Sew remaining seams; weave in all ends.

Sheep in the Meadow Cardigan

For Materials List See Page 20, Directions Page 23

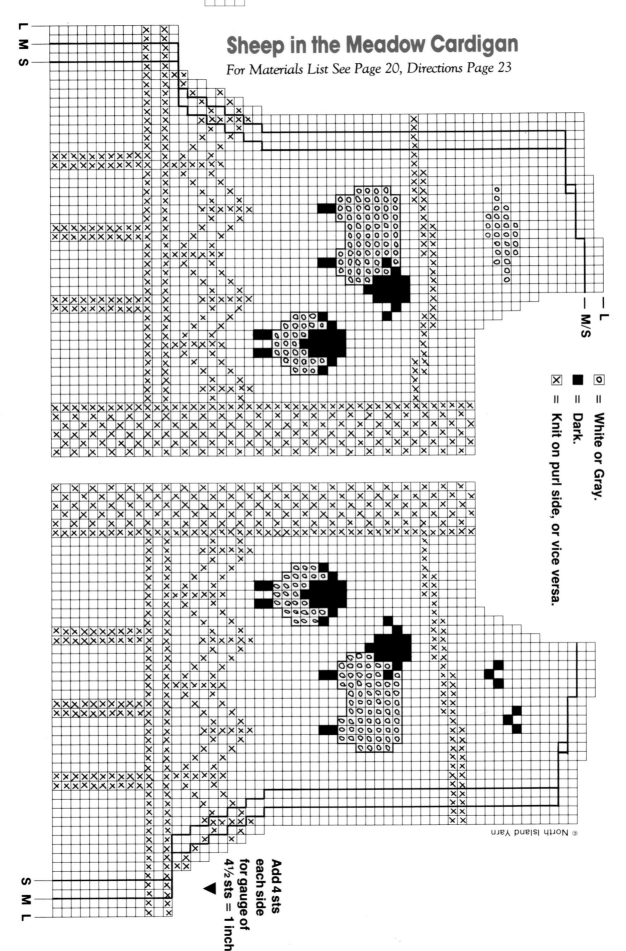

— L

— M/S

◙ = White or Gray.

■ = Dark.

☒ = Knit on purl side, or vice versa.

© North Island Yarn

▲ Add 4 sts each side for gauge of 4½ sts = 1 inch

Versatile Cable Cardigan

This variation on our cable sweater accommodates the many knitters who prefer cardigans. This pattern will fit the split graphs for the Sheep in the Meadow, Sailboat and Appletree sweaters.

Needles: US 5 and 9—or whatever size needed to get stitch gauge of 4 sts = 1 inch.
Buttons: 6 Pewter Buttons
Sizes: 36(38,40)

Back

With smaller needles, cast on 72 (75,81) sts. Work K2,P1 ribbing for 3¼ inches incr 6 (7,5) sts evenly in last row—78(82,86) sts. Change to larger needles and proceed as follows:

Row 1: K8(10,12),P2,K6,P2,K6,P2,K26, P2,K6,P2,K6,P2,K8(10,12).

Row 2: P8(10,12),K2,P6,K2,P6,K2,P26, K2,P6,K2,P6,K2,P8(10,12).

Rows 3,5: Same as Row 1.

Rows 4,6: Same as Row 2.

Row 7: K8(10,12),P2,C6b (do this cable by slipping 3 sts to holder, hold in back of work, K3,K3 from holder), P2,C6b,P2,K26, P2,C6f (do this by slipping 3 sts to holder, hold in front of work, K3,K3 from holder), P2,C6f,P2,K8(10,12).

Rows 8,10,12,14: Same as Row 2.

Rows 9,11,13: Same as Row 1.

Row 15: Repeat Row 7.

Continue knitting the knit sts and purling the purl sts with no more cabling until work measures 11½ (12,12) inches, or 2½ inches less than desired length to underarm. Repeat rows 7-15, then rows 2 and 3 once. With wrong side facing you, knit the next three rows to create two ridges on right side of work. The rest of the back is worked in stockinette stitch. *Armholes:* Bind off 5 sts at the beg of the next 2 rows—68(72,76) sts. Decrease 1 st each and every other row 5 times—58(62,66) sts. Work 32(32,34) more rows. Bind off 5(6,7) sts at shoulder edge next 4 rows; bind off 6 sts beg next 2 rows. Place center 26 sts on holder.

Left Front

With smaller needles, cast on 41(44,47) sts. Work K2,P1 ribbing on first 36(39,42) sts, then seed-stitch (K1,P1,K1,P1,K1) on remaining 5 sts. Next row: K1,P1,K1,P1,K1 first 5 sts, then K1,P2 across row. Continue in ribbing for 3¼ inches; incr 3(2,1) sts evenly across last row of ribbing. Change to larger needles, K10(12,14),P2,K6,P2,K6,P2, K10,P1,K1, P1,K1,P1,K1. Work cables the same as back and continue on up, keeping 5 sts in seed-stitch for center-front button band. When ridges are completed, decrease for armhole same as back and *start chart (p. 22, p.25 or p. 29)* for *Left Front.* Work neck as follows: Place 14 sts on holder, then decr 1 st at neck edge every other row 4 times. Decrease for shoulder to correspond with Back.

Right Front

Work same as Left Front, only mirror image, and allow 6 buttonholes evenly spaced on seed-stitch button band. *To work a buttonhole: work to within 4 sts of end of row, bind off 2 sts firmly, finish row. Next row, cast on 2 sts firmly over bound-off sts to make buttonhole.* The first buttonhole should be halfway up ribbing; the last one, in neck ribbing; the others, evenly spaced in between.

Sleeves

With smaller needles, cast on 39(39,42) sts. Work K2,P1 ribbing for 3¼ inches, incr 3(5,4) sts evenly across last row of ribbing— 42(44,46) sts. Change to larger needles and work as follows. Row 1: K12(13,14),P2,K6, P2,K6,P2,K12(13,14). Continue working the cables as for front and back while increasing 1 st each side every 8th row 7 times—56(58,60) sts. Work until sleeve measures 14½ inches, or 2½ inches less than desired length to underarm. Twist cables again and work ridges. *Sleeve Cap:* bind off 5 sts beg next 2 rows; dec 1 st each end every other row until 24 sts remain. Bind off 3 sts beg next 4 rows; bind off remaining sts.

Finishing

Sew shoulder seams. Pick up and knit approx 78 sts including sts from holders, and work K2,P1 ribbing (first row is K1,P2) for 1 inch, working last buttonhole in the proper place. Bind off. Sew remaining seams; weave in ends. Sew on buttons.

Sailboat Sweater

Materials (for pattern p. 21):
Wool Knitting Worsted, 4 sts = 1 in.
5 (4oz) skeins Main Color
100 yds Sky Color
2 yds Boat Color
20 yds Spruce Green—Trees

Materials (for pattern p. 64):
Cotton or Cotton/Wool, 4½ sts = 1 in
1200 yds Main Color
100 yds Sky Color
2 yds Boat Color
20 yds Spruce Green—Trees

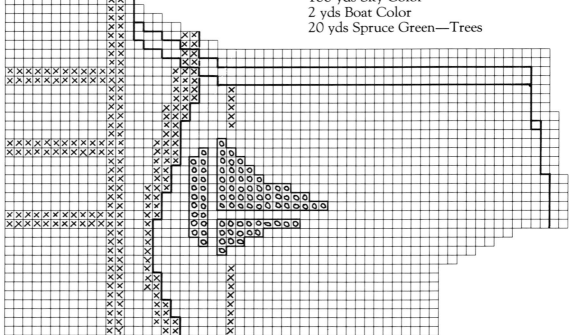

O = White.

∖ = Green.

☒ = Purl instead of knit, or vice versa.

Add 4 sts each side for gauge of 4½ sts = 1 inch

◄

Sailboat Cardigan

(Pattern p. 23)
(Materials p. 24)

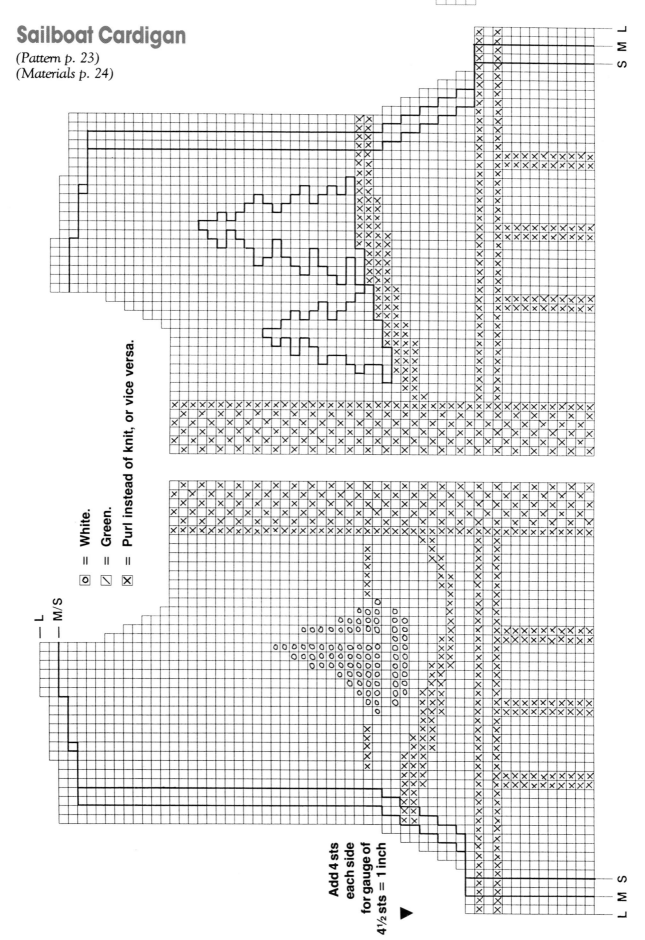

○ = White.

╲ = Green.

✕ = Purl instead of knit, or vice versa.

Add 4 sts
each side
for gauge of
4½ sts = 1 inch

Appletree Pullover

Sailboat Pullover

Appletree Pullover

Materials (for pattern p. 21):
Wool Knitting Worsted, 4 sts = 1 in.
5 (4oz) skeins Medium Blue
20 yds Natural
20 yds Dark Sheeps Gray
20 yds Dark Green
75 yds Light Green for Field
3 yds Red
3 yds Yellow

Materials (for pattern p. 64):
Cotton or Cotton Wool, 4½ sts = 1 in.
1200 yds Main Color
20 yds Natural
20 yds Dark Brown
20 yds Dark Green
75 yds Light Green for Field
3 yds Red
3 yds Yellow

⊠ = Knit on purl side, purl on knit side.
⊞ = Gold.
■ = Brown.
⊡ = White.

Field = Light Green.
Fence & Sky = Main Color.
Tree Foliage = Dark Green.
⚡ = French Knots (done afterward).

◀ Add 4 sts each side for gauge of 4½ sts = 1 inch

Appletree Cardigan

(Pattern p. 23)
(Materials p. 28)

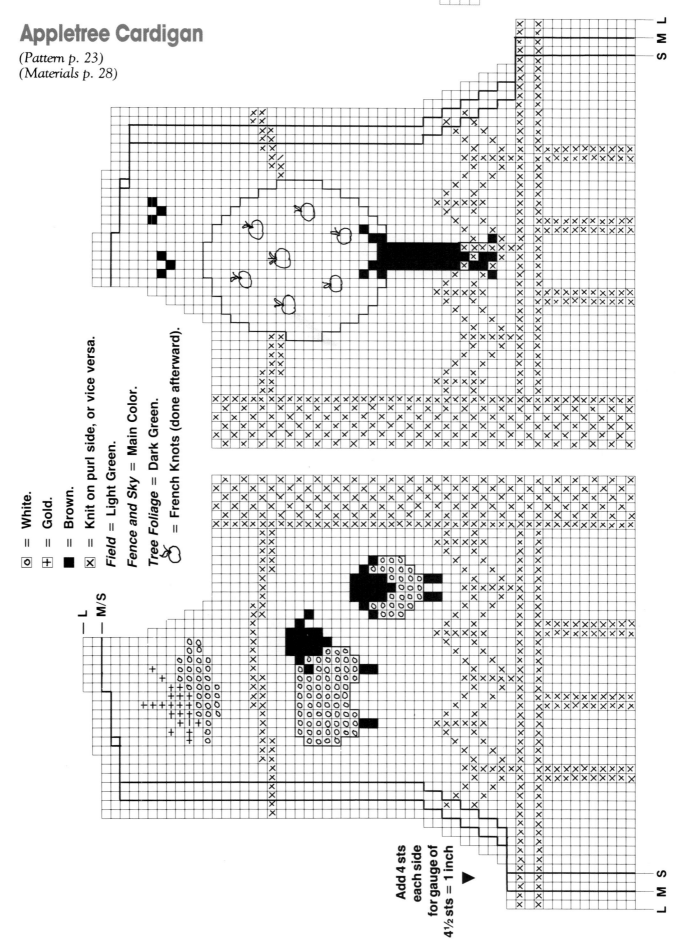

◙ = White.

⊞ = Gold.

■ = Brown.

☒ = Knit on purl side, or vice versa.

Field = Light Green.

Fence and Sky = Main Color.

Tree Foliage = Dark Green.

🍎 = French Knots (done afterward).

Add 4 sts
each side
for gauge of
4½ sts = 1 inch ▶

Raising Sheep on Islands

Islands have long been an inspiration for knitters and designers because they have long been a home to sheep. Rugged creatures, sheep are able to graze on relatively sparse pasture and survive the often harsh seasons to which the islands are subjected. Sheep populations on islands have undergone a small revival in recent years, although numbers are nowhere near the estimated high of 20,000 at the turn of the century.

In its time sheep farming was a major source of income to many of the islands. On our island in 1858 the census included over 2000 sheep. Steamships traveled routinely between the islands (with the cargo often reaching Boston in 24 hours!) and so the highly prized native lamb had a regular trip to market. Fleeces, considered to be of better quality than those from the mainland, have continued to be rewarded with a premium price. It is thought that the higher quality is a result of the alternate cycles of sunshine and dampness (fog and rainy weather) which produce a cleaner wool with a good staple full of crimp.

As well as living on the larger islands, over the years, sheep have been kept on many of the small, uninhabited islands which abound in the bay, and they can still be found on a few of these islands. Some are out there year round and rounded up twice a year—once for shearing, hoof trimming and castrating in the spring and again in the fall to collect the male lambs. Most farmers bring their sheep back to the barn for the winter—having them closer at hand to observe lambing. The animals are transported by boat, not always an easy task.

On these islands the shore provides the fencing and dogs and coyotes are rarely the problem they are on the mainland. Since sheep can receive most of their moisture from the dew and what is in the grass they eat, providing water is not the major prob-

lem it is for other farm animals. Foraging for seaweed that is a part of the sheep's diet, increases their adaptability in dry summers. The fleeces are generally cleaner when sheep are not raised in a barnyard and the sheep are also less troubled by parasites such as intestinal worms and ticks.

Although it sounds like an ideal arrangement, managing island sheep is not without it's pitfalls. Catching the sheep, whether for the semiannual routines or to move them to another island, can be very tricky even on a small island. Sheep are by nature suspicious and, after being left in the wild for extended periods, even common standbys such as rattling a bucket of grain are useless for catching them. Many returning caravans of sheep are short one or two members who became "wild" sheep, possibly to be caught on the next round. On occasion, such as a particularly sparse November deer hunting season, members of the flock will be missing—appropriated by poachers to replace the sought after wild deer.

Spring Scene Cardigan

This popular cardigan was inspired by a trip through the Pennsylvania mountains to visit my old friend Norma. Waking up in the morning and looking across the rolling hills at the orchards in blossom left me so inspired that I couldn't stop graphing the design during the whole car ride back to Maine. The combination of the challenge to the knitter and the simplicity of style has made this our all time most popular design.

Needle: Size 8—24″ circular needle—or whatever size needed to get a stitch gauge of 4½ sts = 1 in.
Bobbins: 2 packs
Size: 34(36,38,40)
Materials: (The trick is getting all of the colors to harmonize).
5 (4 oz.) skeins Sky Blue
1 (4 oz.) skein Dark Green
100 yds Green Heather
30 yds Fir Green (lighter than Green Heather)
30 yds Light Green
25 yds Natural White
25 yds Dark Brown
15 yds Pink
10 yds Red Heather
10 yds Yellow
Buttons: 6 Pewter Buttons

Popcorn Stitch: K1,P1,K1,P1,K1 in the same stitch and then loop 4 stitches over the first as if binding off.
Seed Stitch: K1,P1,K1,P1 across the row. Next row is worked the same, so that you knit the purl stitches and purl the knit stitches.

Body

Cast on 166(174,182,190) sts on circular needle using bottom color of chart. When doing knit side, work chart right to left; purl side goes left to right. Decide on length of sweater now so that buttonhles will be evenly spaced. The first buttonhole is worked at the end of the 6th row. [To make buttonhole: purl to within 5 sts of end, bind off 5th and 4th sts. Work to end. Next row, cast on 2 sts above bound-off stitches.] Cardigan length from underarm will be approx 13 inches if buttonholes are worked every 3⅜ inches, or approx 15 inches if worked every 3¾ inches. Work chart starting at right side working to the left, using bobbins so you don't have to carry colors. Work to armhole, ending on wrong side.

—CENTER FRONT

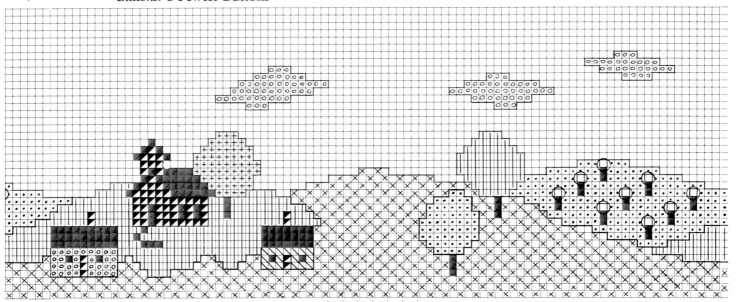

40
38
36
34

Armholes

Next row: Knit 38(40,42,44) sts, bind off next 10 sts for armhole. Work 70(74,78, 82) sts for back, bind off 10 sts for armhole. Work 38(40,42,44) sts for other front. Purl next row, attaching balls of yarn where needed. Next row: dec 1 st each side of armhole this row, and again next 4 knit rows (5 times in all). Continue till armhole measures 5 inches (about 3 rows beyond last buttonhole): end on wrong side.

Neck

Bind off 12 sts beginning next two rows. Dec 1 st each side of neck every other row 4 times. Work till armhole is 7½(7 ½,8,8,) inches. Bind off as follows:

Size 34: Bind off 6 sts at armhole edge next 4 rows, then 5 sts next 2 rows.

Size 36: Bind off 6 sts at armhole edge next 4 rows, then 7 sts next 2 rows.

Size 38: Bind off 7 sts at armhole edge next 6 rows.

Size 40: Bind off 8 sts at armhole edge next 4 rows, then 7 sts next 2 rows.

Then bind off 26 sts of back neck. Sew shoulders from right side, matching stitch for stitch.

Green Heather (Seed Stitch)

Sleeves

Cast on 42(44,44,46) sts. Work in stockinette stitch for 2 inches. Incr 1 st each side every 8th row 6 times—54(56,56,58) sts until 16(16½,16½,17) inches or desired length to underarm. Bind off 5 sts beginning next 2 rows. Dec 1 st each end every knit row till 20 sts remain. Bind off 2 sts beginning next 4 rows. Bind off remaining 12 sts.

Trim

Trim is worked in stockinette stitch. Cast on 6 sts of contrasting color. Work a long-enough strip to go around sweater's bottom, up fronts, and around neck. Also knit two strips for cuffs of sleeves. To attach, put right sides together and use a back stitch. Take a ¼″ tuck in trim for a nice sharp corner. Trim will curl around. Slip stitch on wrong side if you wish. Block pieces, sew seams right-side together using back stitch. Weave in ends. Sew on buttons.

☑	= **White.**	⊞	= **Dark Green.**
☐	= **Fir Green.**	◨	= **Yellow.**
⊡	= **Light Green.**	◪	= **Red.**
■	= **Dark Brown.**	⬭	= **Pink Popcorn Stitches.**

—CENTER FRONT

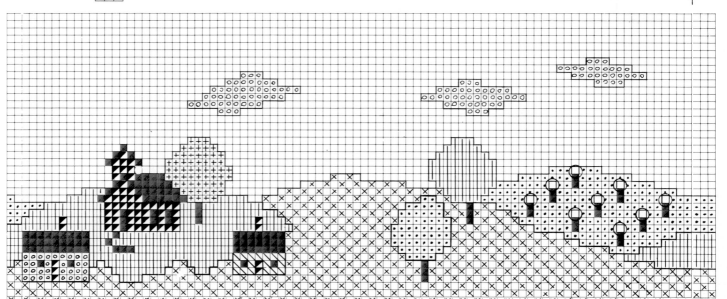

40
38
36
34

Spring Scene Cardigan

Fall Scene Cardigan

Fall Scene Cardigan

A scene from a grey fall day on the island—many colors of the trees, the grass turning brown and a boat crossing the bay on a day when the water is bluer than at any other time of year.

Needle: Size 8—24″ circular needle—or whatever size needed to get stitch gauge of 4½ sts = 1 in.
Bobbins: 2 packs
Size: 34(36,38,40)
Materials:
5 (4 oz) skeins Light Sheeps Gray
1 (4 oz) skein Dark Green
75 yds Medium Olive Green (Bracken)
25 yds Natural White
25 yds Tan
20 yds Medium Blue
15 yds Red Heather
15 yds Gold
10 yds Dark Brown
Buttons: 6 Pewter Buttons

Body

Cast on 166(174,182,190) sts on circular needle using bottom color of chart. When doing knit side, work chart right to left. Purl side goes left to right. Decide on length of sweater now so that buttonhles will be evenly spaced. The first buttonhole is worked at the end of the 6th row. [To make buttonhole: purl to within 5 sts of end, bind off 5th and 4th stitches. Work to end. Next row, cast on 2 sts above bound-off stitches.] Cardigan length from underarm will be approx 13 inches if buttonholes are worked every 3⅜ inches, or approx 15 inches if worked every 3¾ inches. Work chart starting at right side working to the left, using bobbins so you don't have to carry colors. Work to armhole, ending on wrong side.

Armholes

Next row: Knit 38(40,42,44) sts, bind off next 10 sts for armhole. Work 70(74,78,82) sts for back, bind off 10 sts for armhole. Work 38(40,42,44) sts for other front. Purl next row, attaching balls of yarn where needed. Next row: dec 1 st each side of armhole this row, and again next 4 knit rows (5 times in all). Continue till armhole measures 5 inches (about 3 rows beyond last buttonhole): end on wrong side.

CENTER FRONT

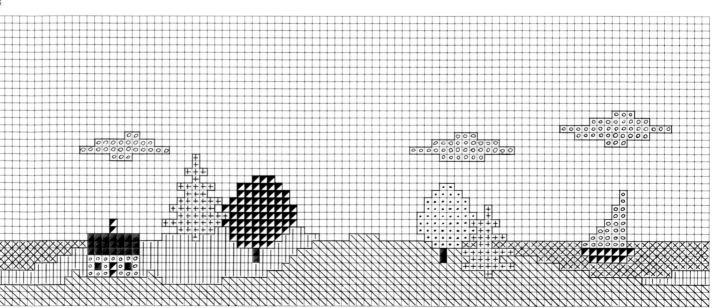

40
38
36
34

Neck

Bind off 12 sts beginning next two rows. Dec 1 st each side of neck every other row 4 times. Work till armhole is 7½(7½,8,8,) inches. Bind off as follows:

Size 34: Bind off 6 sts at armhole edge next 4 rows, then 5 sts next 2 rows.

Size 36: Bind off 6 sts at armhole edge next 4 rows, then 7 sts next 2 rows.

Size 38: Bind off 7 sts at armhole edge next 6 rows.

Size 40: Bind off 8 sts at armhole edge next 4 rows, then 7 sts next 2 rows.

Then bind off 26 sts of back neck. Sew shoulders from right side, matching stitch for stitch.

Sleeves

Cast on 42(44,44,46) sts. Work in stockinette stitch for 2 inches. Incr 1 st each side every 8th row 6 times—54(56,56,58) sts, until 16(16½,16½,17) inches or desired length to underarm. Bind off 5 sts beginning next 2 rows. Dec 1 st each end every knit row till 20 sts remain. Bind off 2 sts beginning next 4 rows. Bind off remaining 12 sts.

Trim

Trim is worked in stockinette stitch. Cast on 6 sts of contrasting color. Work a long-enough strip to go around sweater's bottom, up fronts, and around neck. Also knit two strips for cuffs of sleeves. To attach, put right sides together and use a back stitch. Take a ¼″ tuck in trim for a nice sharp corner. Trim will curl around. Slip stitch on wrong side if you wish. Block pieces, sew seams right-side together using back stitch. Weave in ends. Sew on buttons.

◪ = Red.

◙ = Yellow.

■ = Brown.

◩ = Bracken.

◉ = White.

⊞ = Dark Green.

⊠ = Blue.

⊓ = Tan.

—CENTER FRONT

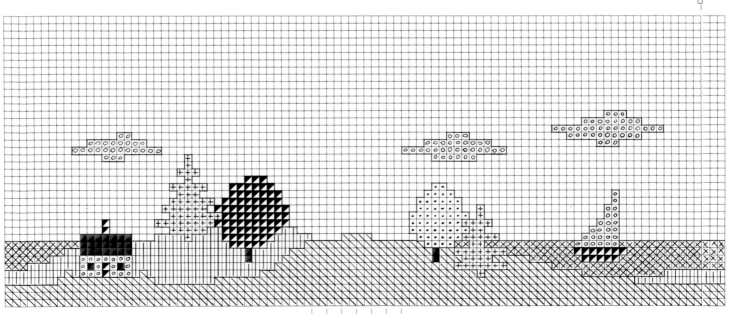

40
38
36
34

Life in an Island Town

Although there are many similarities between island life and that in any small town, there are many obvious and a few subtle differences, the most striking being a considerable amount of water separating us from the "mainland." Along with this goes a perception of oneself as an island resident. A local writer said that people on the mainland don't generally regard themselves as "mainlanders" but Islanders see them as such and themselves as Islanders.

Our town has between 350 and 400 year round residents depending on the year and who is counting. In the summer this number swells to an estimated 2500. Indians are known to have lived here as long ago as 3300 BC, but the beginnings of the current settlement date back to around 1760, with "summer people" arriving in the late 1800's.

Geographically, the island is three miles wide by eight miles long and it is located in a bay where it is surrounded by several other islands of many sizes, both inhabited and not. The terrain is predominately covered with red spruce which grew up as the pastures of earlier times were abandoned. Some of the fields still remain open and flourish with wildflowers in the spring and early summer. The shoreline is a reflection of long past volcanic and glacial activity, leaving behind dramatic ledges and rocky beaches.

Fishing and farming reigned in the early days of the island and continued to be a strong part of the economic foundation through the early 1900's, the island now derives a major part of its income through businesses that serve the summer people. The construction and service trades thrive and two boatyards provide repairs, maintenance and new boat construction. Full time fisherman are rare but there are many who fish for lobsters or scallops in addition to their various other jobs. Some of the other

nearby islands have a reversed economic base—fishing as the backbone with the summer trades secondary.

The town itself is clustered near the ferry landing, the social center of an island's life. "Downtown" consists of a general store, gas station and boatyard, post office, library and a few seasonal gift shops. The ferry travels to the mainland from one to three times a day, depending on the day of the week and the season. Sometimes the boat is met by no one, but more often many gather to see who is going off or returning. All vehicles and their cargos are scrutinized and new faces are discussed to place their origin.

The ferry ride itself plays a unique role in island life as it is an inescapable fact of residing in an island town. The hour and ten minute ride, which can be rough in bad weather, is on a nearly thirty year old boat which holds approximately 9 cars on deck and thirty or more passengers in the cabin. Although many people stay in their cars, others often choose to ride in the cabin with those traveling on foot. Here gossip is shared, politics are discussed (local, usually) and adversaries are occasionally required to sit closer than they may prefer. Arguments are started and settled or there may be a pleasant conversation between folks who—in another sort of town—might never have had any contact.

There are other qualities that are subtle but are, nonetheless, a critical part of the fabric of life. It is a relatively safe place—people rarely come and go unnoticed. Crime is uncommon as everyone knows almost everyone else. Houses are left unlocked, keys are left in cars and children wander freely, with no distrust of strangers. Not to paint a utopia; rare incidents of vandalism and theft do occur—sometimes they are a local way of getting a message across to the victim. And of course, the down side to our careful observance of each other is that anonymity is unheard of and privacy can be rare—any "news" takes only hours to spread throughout the town.

The island is home to many good cooks, and people meet in each other's homes, often on weekends, to share a meal and keep up on each other's activities. The few restaurants here operate mostly on a seasonal basis, the "Chat and Chew" is the lone winter gathering spot for coffee breaks and lunch. Throughout the year singers, musicians and other entertainers venture across the bay to present their talents for an occasional island cultural event. A school play, two or three dances and the customary community celebrations marking such holidays as Memorial Day and the Fourth of July usually round out the year's organized activities.

The school, which is the smallest K through 12th grade school in the state, has an average class size hovering around 4 or 5 (sometimes there is only one student, which makes for quite an unusual graduation). It requires a tremendous amount of effort on the part of the school administration, staff and town to maintain an institution that is

an anomaly to the rest of the world. Community members readily turn out and cook for bake sales, volunteer for school projects and follow the basketball team, which sometimes makes it to the state tournaments.

Although the school is often the source of controversy, it is also the source of great pride and participation. The town would likely fade and die were the school to close.

Christmas on the island personifies the warm times in the community. Lights are strung through the town and all of the organizations cooperate to sponsor a big sale of their handiwork in the community building. Residents have parties for friends and families throughout the season and the small post office is busy mailing and receiving boxes. On the last day of school before vacation the children have a party usually with the addition of a skit and are presented with gifts from a local organization handed out, of course, by Santa.

The Sunday School (of the one active island Church) with children in their best clothes performing well practiced songs provides the last organized gathering of the season. Again, a visit from Santa (the children are always a little suspicious by then) who hands out presents, mysteriously knows their names and takes the brave ones in turn on his lap. On that night, it seems like a very safe place where little change could ever come.

Appletree with Sheep Vest

Two weeks before a New England Trades Show, Ralph, our Massachusetts sales representative called to say that he needed something new. Knowing that knitters loved anything with sheep and that many people had felt we needed a cooler alternative to our pullover sweaters, this vest seemed to be just what was called for!

Sizes: 34(36,38,40,42,44).
Needles: US 5 and 8—or whatever size needed to get a stitch gauge of 4½ sts = 1 in.
Materials:
3 (4 oz) skeins Light Sheeps Gray
90 yds Light Green
90 yds Sky Blue
7 yds Red
7 yds Yellow
15 yds Green Heather
25 yds Dark Sheep Gray
25 yds Natural White

Front

With smaller needles and using main color (MC), cast on 72(76,80,84,88,92) sts. Work in ribbing of K1,P1, for 22 rows. At the end of last row of ribbing, incr 1 st. Change to larger needles and work as follows:

Row 1 (and all right-side rows except cable rows): K10(12,14,16,18,20),P2,K4, P2,K2, work chart on next 33 sts, K2,P2, K4,P2,K10(12,14,16,18,20).

Row 2 (and all wrong-side rows): P10 (12,14,16,18,20),K2,P4,K2,P2, work chart on next 33 sts, P2,K2,P4,K2,P10(12,14,16, 18,20).

Row 3 (and every 6th row afterward): K10(12,14,16,18,20),P2,C4b (do this cable by slipping 2 sts to a double-pointed needle, hold in back of work, K2,K2 sts from dp needle), P2,K2, work chart (33 sts), K2,P2, C4b,P2,K10(12,14,16,18,20).

Continue in this manner, incr one st each side every 16th row, 3 times. Work until piece measures 13 inches or desired length to underarm. If chart needs to be lengthened or shortened, do so at top. End on wrong side.

Armhole

Bind off 6(8,9,11,12,14) sts at beginning of next 2 rows. Dec 1 st each end every other row 5(5,6,6,7,7) times. *Neck Shaping:* When chart is completed (armhole will measure about 2½ inches), on the right side, work center 33 sts in the following way: knit 4 sts in chart color (CC), 25 sts in MC, 4CC. Next row: purl 3CC, 27MC, 3CC. Next row: K2CC, K2MC, place 25 sts on holder, attach another ball of yarn, K2MC, K2CC. Next row: purl 1CC, purl 1MC, purl 2 tog MC. Work other side to correspond. Continue to dec 1 st each side neck edge using MC three more times until 12 sts remain each side. Continue working cables until armhole measures 7½ (8,8,8½,8½,9) inches. Bind off.

Back

Work same as front except work center 33 sts in stockinette stitch using MC. Work until armhole is ½ inch more than front before working neck decreases.

Finishing

When back and front are completed, sew them together at shoulders, matching sts. Using a 24-inch circular #5 needle, pick up and knit 3 out of 4 available sts plus sts on holders, around neck. Work 2(2,2,3,3,3,) rows ribbing (K1,P1). Bind off. Sew side seams right sides together using a back stitch. Work ribbing around armholes to match neck. Weave in ends.

Appletree with Sheep Vest

Appletree with Sheep Vest

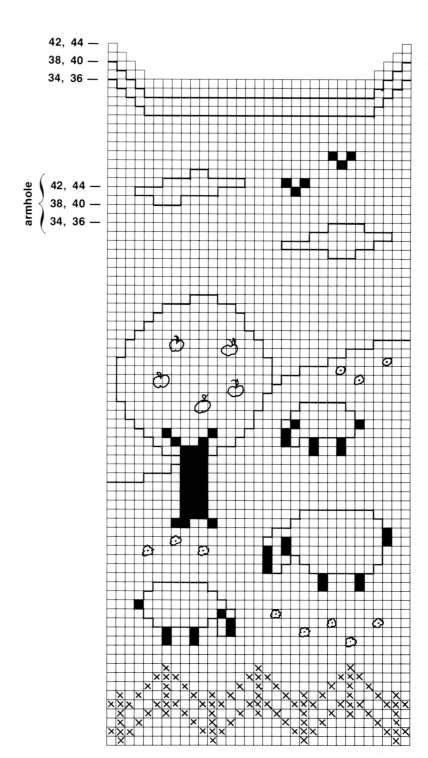

■ = Brown.

Clouds & Sheep = White.

Hill = Pale Green.

Tree Foliage = Dark Green.

Fence = Main Color .

Sky = Blue.

Apples = Red (French Knots).

Flowers = Yellow (French Knots).

Sunset Over the Camden Hills Vest

A design inspired by our view of the sunset from a popular spot called Tar Tank Beach, named because a big tank used to sit there. This very narrow part of the island is a favorite sunset watching spot. In the old days a large scow used to pull up on the beach and pump tar into the tank for use in maintaining the thirty miles of roads that circle and cross the island. (Mileage builds up very slowly on a car that lives out here.)

Sizes: 34(36,38,40,42,44).
Needles: US 5 and 8—or whatever size needed to get a stitch gauge of 4½ sts = 1 in.
Materials:
3 (4 oz) skeins Jade Heather
75 yds Light Heather
50 yds Blue-green
20 yds Denim Blue
20 yds Dark Green
20 yds Natural White

Front

With smaller needles and using main color (MC), cast on 72 (76,80,84,88,92) sts. Work in ribbing of K1,P1, for 22 rows. At the end of last row of ribbing, incr 1 st. Change to larger needles and work as follows:

Row 1 (and all right-side rows except cable rows): K10(12,14,16,18,20), P2,K4, P2,K2, work chart on next 33 sts, K2,P2, K4,P2,K10(12,14,16,18,20).

Row 2 (and all wrong-side rows): P10 (12,14,16,18,20),K2,P4,K2,P2, work chart on next 33 sts, P2,K2,P4,K2,P10(12,14,16, 18,20).

Row 3 (and every 6th row afterward): K10(12,14,16,18,20), P2,C4b (do this cable by slipping 2 sts to a double-pointed needle, hold in back of work, K2,K2 sts from dp needle), P2,K2, work chart (33 sts), K2, P2,C4b,P2,K10(12,14,16,18,20).

Continue in this manner, incr 1 st each side every 16th row, 3 times. Work until piece measures 13 inches or desired length to underarm. If chart needs to be lengthened or shortened, do so at top. End on wrong side.

Armhole

Bind off 6(8,9,11,12,14) sts at beginning of next 2 rows. Dec 1 st each end every other row 5(5,6,6,7,7,) times. *Neck shaping:* When chart is completed (armhole will measure about 2½"), on the right side, work center 33 sts in the following way: Knit 4 sts in chart color (CC), 25 sts in MC, 4CC. Next row: purl 3CC, 27MC, 3CC. Next row: K2CC, K2MC, place 25 sts on holder, attach another ball of yarn, K2MC, K2CC. Next row: purl 1CC, purl 1 MC, purl 2 tog MC. Work other side to correspond. Continue to dec 1 st each side neck edge using MC three more times until 12 sts remain each side. Continue working cables until armhole measures 7½(8,8,8½,8½,9) inches. Bind off.

Back

Work same as front except work center 33 sts in stockinette stitch using MC. Work until armhole is ½ inch more than front before working neck decreases.

Finishing

When back and front are completed, sew them together at shoulders, matching sts. Using a 24-inch circular #5 needle, pick up and knit 3 out of 4 available sts plus sts on holders, around neck. Work 2(2,2,3,3,3,) rows ribbing (K1,P1). Bind off. Sew side seams right sides together using a back stitch. Work ribbing around armholes to match neck. Weave in ends.

Sunset Over the Camden Hills Vest

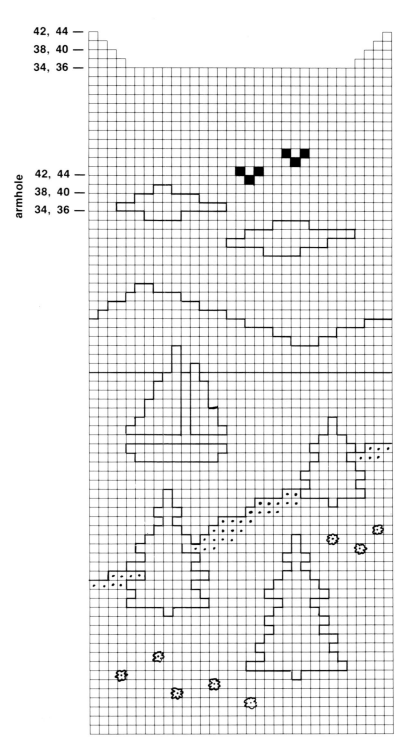

42, 44 —
38, 40 —
34, 36 —

armhole

42, 44 —
38, 40 —
34, 36 —

☐ = Purl instead of knit, or vice versa.

Clouds & Sailboat = White.

Trees & Birds = Dark Green.

Hills = Purple.

Sky = Warm Heather.

Field = Main Color.

Water = Blue.

Flowers = French Knots worked
  in sky color.

Sunset Over the Camden Hills Vest

History of the Business

How North Island Designs Came to Be—
as told by Chellie

This story begins in the summer of 1977 when a knitting business was a far cry from my mind or daily chores. Charlie, my husband, and our daughter Hannah, age one, and I were living in a rented farm in the middle of the island. It had a warm southern slope and a view of the Fresh Pond, the island water supply. Since my background was in horticulture and I had been involved in the organic gardening movement, we were busily trying to establish ourselves as farmers. Over the next three years I managed a 2 acre market garden, selling vegetables in a makeshift store in our shed and in town out of the VW van. Selling out of the back of the van was my first experience in customer frenzy—in a town where garden fresh produce was in scarce supply, even the most polite could be seen nudging their way to the head of the line.

Wanting to have more of a farm, we gradually added several varieties of animals. It began with dairy cows—we got to know several quite well before we were done. There were many mornings while I was milking when Hannah sat in her playpen in the warm, manure stained old barn. I kept a watchful eye on the foot belonging to a Guernsey cow named Audrey—just waiting for the moment when it casually found its way into the bucket. There are some things you just can't strain out.

Cows led to chickens, pigs and, of course, sheep. Sheep being the traditional island animal, we could not be long without them. In early years we sheared our flock of 6 or 8 by hand, using scissor-like shears. It has been said that a sheep can die on its back in the hands of a slow shearer. Luckily, although some of them spent 45 minutes (it takes a good shearer about 2 or 3 minutes, with modern equipment) in that uncomfortable position, all survived. Sheep myth includes the generally accepted fact that

although sheep will always put up an initial struggle, they soon give up and are yours to do what you will.

Naturally, this abundance of fleece led to another project. Since I wasn't a hand spinner (hadn't even learned to knit yet), we did what many New England small farmers do—we packed up the fleece in grain bags and mailed it to Bartlettyarns in Harmony, Maine. They, in turn, returned an appropriate amount of already spun yarn in trade—(usually 55% to account for the loss to oil, chaff and other waste).

Now, what was a non-knitter going to do with all of this yarn? It seemed as if everyone on the island knit, so for the right price, many became good customers. We had an attic full of yarn that people came to visit in the winter and by the next summer we were selling yarn in the farm stand. (By then we had given up the trips to town—we had plenty of customers willing to wait for us to run out to the field for that freshly cut lettuce).

Many of my neighbors had been busy knitting with all this lovely yarn and as these things will, their production began to get a little out of hand. So, we opened up the spare room next to the shed and began selling knitting accessories and pattern books as well as hand knit sweaters, socks and mittens on consignment.

Business was booming, but external circumstances had changed, and it was time for a reevaluation. Another child, Cecily, had come along and a third (Asa) was on his way. The rented farm had been a wonderful home, but we had been building a home of our own on the eastern side of the island and time to move was fast approaching. Our new property was overgrown with the red spruce that covers most of the thin-soiled land on the island, and starting another farm right away was out of the question. With several women busily knitting and an abundance of yarn to sell, I decided to do what any latent entrepreneur would—open a shop in town.

Luckily for me a pretty red house with gingerbread trim was available in just the right location in town and we made plans to inhabit it. Marion, an island resident whose family had been kind to us 11 years earlier when we arrived on the island and who has been a friend ever since, agreed to be my first employee and we were set. We opened our retail store in July of 1982. In addition to knitted goods and supplies and yarn we sold t-shirts, the financial foundation of many small businesses in communities with seasonal populations.

The following year we moved into a more conventional space across the street (Main Street). The building had been the meeting hall of the Knights of Pythias, a secret society that had thrived for years on the island in the days before TV. Although what they did at their meetings is still a secret, when we moved into the building the upstairs space revealed large velvet covered chairs and pedestals, colored lights on the high ceiling and closets full of fancy costumes. We imagined amazing rituals. People remembered that the hall was also used for many public dances and meals (our main floor retail space is called the dining room).

Back to the history—the retail operation grew and although we were basically a seasonal operation (June through September) we often traveled to NY or Boston to have small sales of our sweaters in the winter. Production was high with as many as 25 women knitting during the winter while other work was scarce. It was the perfect way for many people to supplement their income—they were experts at the trade to begin with and were probably going to be knitting in much of their free time anyway. It was the type of work that didn't demand a babysitter, nor the missing of a favorite soap opera. The pay wasn't high, but the fringe benefits seemed to make it worthwhile. We kept the store open one day a week, coming in early to build a fire to warm up the room. People were able to exchange finished projects for new, pick up their checks, drink coffee and see what everyone else was doing.

Slowly, two things began to change—one was in my outlook and the other had to do with the Labor Department. I still was not a knitter. I had made a pair of socks for my husband once—one of those gifts where you actually wrap one and a half socks, the second with the needles still attached—and started a Penny Straker sweater that I passed on to Marion to sew together because it didn't seem to fit (I'm not sure she ever finished it either). I certainly was not a knitter in the real sense of the word. I was in the business for the challenge, the sociability, and because I thought it was a genuinely good thing for the community. But somehow, it was growing beyond what a non-knitter should manage. The women were wonderful in supplying their expertise, but if we were to grow we needed a knitter or designer in the management.

Secondly, this was when the Labor Department (prompted by the labor unions) began to single out home knitting as an industry that needed to be regulated. I knew that we could not comply with the stricter regulations and continue to compete in the market. Although I did a lot of research into our options, our time was limited without some major changes. The business was at a turning point: I wanted to continue to be challenged and I also wanted to provide quality work for women at a decent wage. I was faced with a dilemma.

I spoke with several people hoping to find a new idea, or perhaps a partner or someone to take over the business to free me to do other things. (I had, by this time gotten the urge to go back to outside work and was longing to be farming or working in the landscaping business.) Someone recommended Debby Anderson as an enthusiastic knitter and suggested I speak with her. We had met Debby and her family the previous fall at the beginning of the year school picnic that gathers together the 9 teachers, and most of the 65 students and their parents to eat hot dogs and play games on a fall evening.

In the spring of 1984, Debby and her husband Ross had come to the island for a visit, and spent the night at the only inn. At the time they were living in southern Maine and Debby owned a doll shop in Portsmouth, New Hampshire. To put it mildly, life there was considerably different for them. Debby was making beautiful molded felt dolls. These had been very popular and she had opened a store six years earlier to expand her market and create an income for herself during the time when she was a single parent.

As with all small businesses, her store was a 10 hour a day job and a full time mental commitment and Debby found she had very little time for her family (Debby has 5 children, all but one now grown) and the painting and drawing which she had hoped to pursue. After spending one night at the Inn, waking to the sounds of sheep in the field, but little else, the Andersons decided to take a scan of the very slim real estate market. After 24 hours they decided to settle and purchased a small home, in a

move that is very uncharacteristic of new families on the island. They spent the winter settling in to the new way of life that was here.

Luckily for me, Debby was interested when I spoke to her about joining the business. She had thought she was moving to an island to slow down the pace of her business life (she was still commuting to her doll shop once a month), but an entrepreneur at heart as well as a devoted knitter she was intrigued by the possibilities of our partnership. She began by supplying some designs to knit for the summer trade and helped with the management of the retail store. She suggested the idea of sweater kits and designed the Sheep in the Meadow to be our first. This was followed by the Sailboat and then the colorful Appletree design. We were very pleased with their success in our store, which was not hindered by our primitive packaging.

By fall we were wondering if there were sales available beyond our island base. I, of course, still had fantasies of moving back to the outdoor trades, but was going to stay on long enough to get things organized.

With the National Needlework Show coming up in January of 1986 in New York City we decided to go for broke. We planned to have a booth and see if other yarn shops would be interested in selling what we had found to be successful. We printed a brochure of our first 6 designs, priced them, and went to work. We sold far more than we had ever imagined and the rest, as they say, is history.

The company now sells sweater kits to over 1000 stores across the country. We have attended trades shows just about everywhere and have advertised in many of the knitting magazines. We are constantly increasing our base of designs and are delighted to have come to the point that we have enough to produce a book. We hope that you will enjoy knitting these as well as we have enjoyed creating them.

Running a Business from an Island

Running a business on an island is not without its complications. Our daily flow of cargo—mail, UPS, etc., is determined by the weather. High winds and there is no ferry; fog or rain and the single engine plane that delivers the mail onto a grass strip does not fly. Ice in the winter, although less common, can trap the boat—our one hour and ten minute link with the mainland.

The seasonal nature of island work can be a problem as well. In the winter we have employees available in abundance, but when the summer season approaches, life changes to high gear and all hands are busy. Most of the women are out trying to keep up with the myriad of jobs that are available cleaning the large summer houses, gardening, cooking, waiting on tables and many more. Our pace picks up as well, as stores begin to order for the coming knitting and Christmas season.

This contributes to a feeling of frenzy for our business and to the island as well. Islanders are fond of saying that summer is all over on the Fourth of July and there is more than a shred of truth to that. The warm season is short and seems to take so long to prepare for when it finally arrives it slips through your fingers—not unlike finally opening your presents on Christmas morning, you wonder if the anticipation was more than half of the fun.

Our Staff

Over the years some workers have come and gone but Marion, the first, is still with the business. She is an islander of many generations who hates to see island customs change, especially watching the old accents die as a result of outsiders like me who don't properly drop their R's. Cris has been with us since we began making kits and supervises our production, packing and shipping. She is a gardener and has been known to take in laundry in her "spare" time. She is also our fastest knitter and the one we call on when

we need a sample in time for a show. Connie answers the phone and takes the orders and has the difficult job of seeing to it that the customers pay the bills. She is also a nurse and the wife of our island doctor and occasionally has to leave work to assist him.

Vivian is our ever cheerful crew member who puts together our covers, answers brochure requests, keeps us tidy and well organized. Her husband, a 20 year crew member on the ferry takes two and sometimes three rides across the bay every day in almost all kinds of whether. Janice is responsible for much of our bookkeeping, the mailing lists, and waits patiently for the deposits so she can pay the bills. Cheryl helps us out when we get busy, and doubles as the island's ace cake baker for any special occasion. Ann, a family member and summer helper is an invaluable asset for those very busy months.

Debby is in charge of design and production and Chellie handles the challenges of finances and marketing. Being partners is never easy but it allows us take on different parts of the business and overlap when necessary.

Whimsical Chicken Vest

Sizes: 38 (40,42)
Needles: US 5 and 9—or whatever size needed to get stitch gauge of 4 sts = 1 in.
Materials:
4 (4 oz) skeins Main Color
10 yds each Pink & Teal Donegal Tweed for hen
5 yds Yellow for legs & corn
2 yds Plum for combs
Buttons: 6 Pewter Buttons

Back

With smaller needles, cast on 72(78,81) sts. Work K2,P1 ribbing for 4 inches, increasing 7(5,6) sts evenly across last row of ribbing— 79(83,87) sts. Change to larger needles and follow chart for back panel. Work till 13½(14,14½) inches or desired length to underarm. *Armhole:* Bind off 5 sts beginning next 2 rows, then dec 1 st each end every other row 5 times. Work 31(31,33) more rows. Bind off 5(6,7) sts at shoulder edge beg next 4 rows, then 6 sts beg next 2 rows. Place center 27 sts on holder.

Left Front

With smaller needles, cast on 41(44,47) sts. Work K2,P1 ribbing on first 36(39,42) sts, then seed-stitch (K1,P1,K1,P1,K1) on remaining 5 sts. Next row: K1,P1,K1,P1,K1 first 5 sts, then K1,P2 across row. Continue in ribbing for 4 inches, increasing 3(2,1) sts evenly across last row of ribbing. Change to larger needles, and work stockinette st first 13(15,17) sts. Then follow chart for chicken-wire pattern. Work armholes same as back. Work neck as follows: place 14 sts on holder, then dec 1 st at neck edge every other row 4 times. Decrease shoulder to correspond to back.

Right Front

Work same as left front, only a mirror image, and work 6 buttonholes evenly spaced on button band. To work buttonhole: work to within 4 sts of end of row, bind off 2 sts firmly, finish row. Next row, cast on 2 sts over bound-off sts to make buttonhole. First buttonhole should be half-way up ribbing; last buttonhole, midway in neck ribbing; and the other four evenly spaced between.

Finishing

Sew shoulder seams. Using smaller needles, pick up and knit *approx* 78 sts around neck. Work seed-stitch on 5 sts each end, K2,P1 ribbing in between for 1 inch. Don't forget last buttonhole. Bind off loosely.

Armholes

Pick up and knit approx 93(93,96) sts and work ribbing same as neck.
Sew seams, weave in loose ends. Sew on buttons.

Whimsical Chicken Vest

▱ = Teal.

■ = Plum.

◣ = Yellow.

Hen = Pink.

☒ = Knit on purl side, or vice versa.

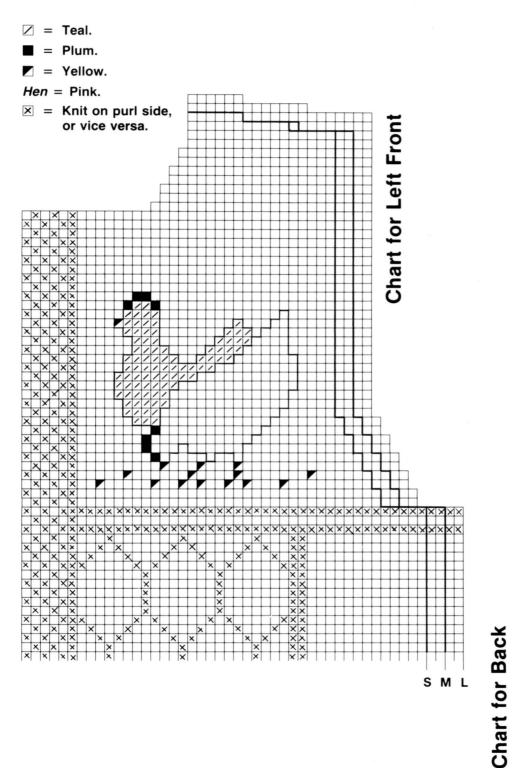

Chart for Left Front

S M L

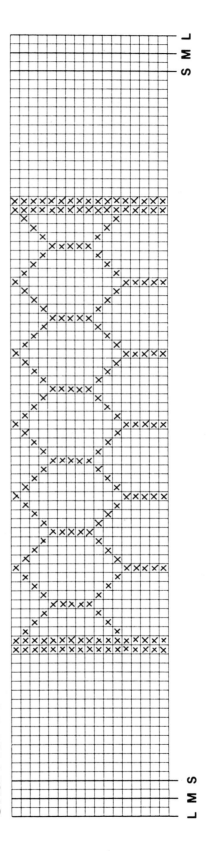

Chart for Back

Summertime Vest

Whimsical Chicken Vest

Summertime Vest

This sweater was designed with the warm weather in mind and was originally done in cotton. The view is through the front porch on a lazy, hot day; sitting in a rocking chair, sipping lemonade, and watching a boat drift by.

Sizes: 34 (36,38,40,42,44).
Needles: US 5 and 8—or whatever size needed to get a stitch-gauge of 4½ sts to the inch.
Materials: Cotton or Cotton Wool
600 yds White
90 yds Green (Grass)
120 yds Blue (Sky & Water)
25 yds Med. Green (Mountain)
5 yds Pink, Yellow and Blue (Flowers)

Front

With smaller needles and using main color (MC), cast on 72(76,80,84,88,92) sts. Work in ribbing of K1,P1, for 22 rows. At the end of last row of ribbing, incr 1 st. Change to larger needles and work as follows:

Row 1 (and all right-side rows except cable rows): K10(12,14,16,18,20),P2,K4, P2,K2, *work chart* on next 33 sts, K2,P2,K4, P2,K10(12,14,16,18,20).

Row 2 (and all wrong-side rows): P10 (12,14,16,18,20),K2,P4,K2,P2, *work chart* on next 33 sts, P2,K2,P4,K2,P10(12,14, 16,18,20).

Row 3(and every 6th row afterward): K10(12,14,16,18,20), P2,C4b (do this cable by slipping 2 sts to a double-pointed needle, hold in back of work, K2,K2 sts from dp needle), P2,K2, *work chart* (33 sts), K2,P2, C4b,P2,K10(12,14,16,18,20).

Continue in this manner, incr 1 st each side every 16th row, 3 times. Work until piece measures 13 inches or desired length to underarm. If chart needs to be lengthened or shortened, do so at top. End on wrong side.

Armhole

Bind off 6(8,9,11,12,14) sts at beginning of next 2 rows. Decr 1 st each end every other row 5(5,6,6,7,7)times. *Neck shaping:* When chart is completed (armhole will measure about 2½"), work 2 rows MC. Next row: work 16 sts, place center 25 sts on holder, attach another ball of yarn, work last 16 sts. On right side dec 1 st at each side of neck edge 4 times (12 sts remain on each side). Continue working cables until armhole measures 7½(8,8,8½,8½,9) inches. Bind off.

Back

Work same as front except work center 33 sts in stockinette stitch using MC. Work until armhole is ½ inch more than front before working neck decreases.

Finishing

When back and front are completed, sew them together at shoulders, matching sts. Using a 24-inch circular #5 needle, pick up and knit 3 out of 4 available sts plus sts on holders, around neck. Work 3 rows ribbing (K1,P1). Bind off. Sew side seams right side together using a back stitch. Work ribbing around armholes to match neck. Weave in ends.

Summertime Vest

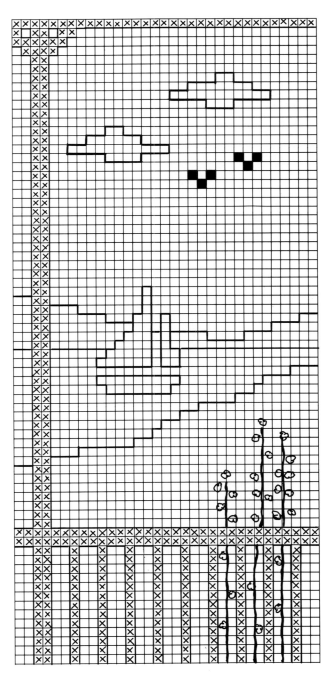

Clouds & Sailboat = White.

Hills & Birds = Medium Green.

Sky & Water = Blue.

Field = Light Green.

Porch Railing = Main Color.

Flowers = French Knots, worked in yellow, pink, & blue. Flower stalks are dark-green Outline Stitch.

Lobsters!!

If not the first question posed when someone hears you live in Maine, then early in the conversation, people will mention the pastime of eating Maine lobster. Most tourists have it on their agenda when visiting the state and a meal of lobsters is certainly a summertime requirement for island residents—year round and seasonal alike.

There are many aspects of a lobster's life that may come as a surprise to the casual diner. To begin with, although it is known that lobsters were enjoyed as early as 1571 in Paris, they were not really commercially fished in Maine until the 1850's. This was in a time when lobsters were so plentiful that they could be found in the seaweed along the shore and were really considered a meal of last resort.

In the beginning lobsters were a minor fishery ranking far behind groundfish, mackerel and herring but now Maine produces one third of the annual catch of lobsters. Today the landings have greatly diminished and there are limits on the size of lobsters that can be taken in hopes of reducing overfishing. It remains a controversial industry, with much discussion taking place annually as to whether or not more regulation is required.

The lobster itself leads a difficult life and a relatively small proportion survive the estimated 7 years it takes to mature to the average size of nine inches that most lobsters are when eaten. The female lobster usually lays between 8000 to 10000 eggs which remain in incubation on the outside of her body for ten or eleven months. Females laden with eggs cannot be kept, by law they must be returned to the sea. Once the young lobsters are swimming on their own, they are heavily preyed upon by many fish including dogfish and cod.

If it survives the early treacherous times, the lobster then proceeds to the busy schedule of molting, the process by which the lobster's shell can accommodate its growing body. In a seemingly impossible feat that takes about five to twenty minutes, the shell splits down the back, in a very straight line, and the lobster completely backs its body out of the shell. (The ghostly shells, perfectly intact, are often brought up in a trap—great for the kids to bring for show and tell at school.) This is accomplished in part because blood has drained out of the claws prior to molting, causing them to shrivel. In spite of this, claws or whole limbs are sometimes lost along the way. After having "shed," the lobster with its new soft shell is extremely vulnerable to predators and will remain in a secluded spot, sometimes for as long as six to eight weeks.

The process of molting or shedding is repeated eight times in the first year, five in the second, and gradually diminishes to as little as once a year as the lobster matures. The female lobster usually mates only in the first twelve hours after molting, and sometimes mature females don't shed every year. This is why emphasis was placed on laws preserving small lobsters, who stand a greater chance of having an opportunity to mate.

Lobsters are primarily scavengers, feeding on dead or decaying matter (think of that the next time you take a bite), although they have been known to eat live fish, dig for clams, feed on algae and eat eel grass. In Maine they are caught by fishermen (and women) in individual wood or metal traps called lobster pots. At the sides of the trap there are two funnels made of net which are the entry point for the lobsters, lured in by the bags of "bait"—usually very fragrant fish which the fisherman has hung in the trap. Once in, the lobster cannot escape and stays there until the fisherman hauls up the trap that is attached to a buoy that floats on the surface of the water. The buoys are painted with each fisherman's identifying colors. A fisherman must tend his traps frequently as lobsters are cannibals and will eat each other if they are confined and hungry. A lobster has the amazing ability to "throw" or cast off a leg or claw if it is grasped by a predator or caught somehow. They can then regenerate a new one, although it will never be as big as the original.

Full time fishermen generally set between 200 to 500 traps, with over half of the licenses issued in Maine going to part time fishermen with less than 100 traps. Although the price in the market usually looks high, making a living from lobstering is a very difficult task. Most fishermen agree that to be successful requires upwards of 300 to 500 traps and most of their income must be made during the four best months of the season. At this scale the investment in gear and a new boat can cost close to $100,000, and with the resulting payments a fisherman must be out working every possible day, in spite of fog, winds and cold. While we are at it we should add that lobstering is dangerous, along with expensive, difficult and competitive—plenty to think about next time you sit down to the tourists' (and many Islander's) favorite meal.

Our Models

Just a few words about all of the very helpful people who willingly brush their hair and put on a clean pair of pants when we call them up at the last minute to pose for the many photos we take in this business. Being on an island we are not in close proximity to many modeling agencies, nor would we be likely to choose to use one if given the opportunity. We are not trying to portray how six foot tall women with fashionable haircuts look in our designs (although we are sure that they would look very well), but are content to use many of the attractive people who live or pass through our community.

On page 15 you will see a photo of Nancy, who is the daughter of Marion, a member of the crew. Nancy manages to look great every time we ask her to model in spite of the fact that she has four children at home, ages six and under. Eliza, on page 35 is a college freshman with an infectious laugh who spent part of last winter in Thailand—a far cry from her winter home of Pennsylvania.

Angela (it's hard to take your eyes off of her picture—page 54) is from an island family with deep roots and is now about to graduate from art school. We have three members of one family modeling, beginning with Christie (page 19) who runs the local inn. Two of her step-children, Amanda (page 18) and Jessie (page 26) appear throughout the book. These girls are in school on the mainland in the winter and work at the inn during the summer.

Shanaugh, a summer resident, spends her days in endless summer as she winters in Hawaii and can be seen with the Siamese cats on page 67. Ankie (page 62), a South African by birth and now an architect in Washington, D.C., was visiting on a photographing day and was willing to give us a few smiles. Chellie, whom you're already familiar with, appears on page 6 with her two oldest children, Hannah and Cecily. Cecily is the one with a piercing look that hides a great imagination. Charlie, their father and a woodworker can be seen on page 7.

Men's Lobster Pullover or Vest

A handsome fisherman and his boat, were the inspiration for this sweater. The design works its way up from the bottom, showing anchors, lobsters, pot buoys from the lobster traps ending with Jade islands on a foggy day. Gulls looking for a handout follow the boat. The blue lobster is no figment of our imagination—perhaps once in a person's lifetime a blue lobster is caught in these waters—cause for great curiosity and conversation.

Remember when you are blocking, to pull the garment down—things that are knit in the round often come out too short and wide, but blocking can cure that.

Sizes: Small (36-38), Medium (40-42), Large (44)
Needles: Sizes 5 and 8 circular (24") for body. Size 5 circular (16") for neck and armhole ribbings.
Sizes 5 and 8 straight.
Gauge: 4½ sts to the inch.
Materials:
4 (4 oz) skeins Main Color (Vest)
7 (4 oz) skeins Main Color (Pullover)
1 (4 oz) skein Natural White
50 yds Dark Green
50 yds Teal

Body

Using smaller 24" circular needle and white, cast on 162 (177,189) sts. Work K2,P1 ribbing for 2 rounds. Then change to main color, work till ribbing measures 3 inches. Incr 6(5,7) sts evenly across next round.

Change to larger needle and start chart. For Large size, work 2 rounds main color before starting design. When you come to Pattern F, Medium and Large sizes need to be modified. For Small size, repeat between A and C. For Medium size, repeat between B and D—there will be 2 extra sts. For Large size, repeat between E and D 6 times—there will be 4 extra sts.

Repeat Pattern E two times. Work 2 rounds main color for Medium and Large sizes.

Armholes

Work 80(86,92) sts, bind off 8(11,12) sts for armhole. Work 76(80,86) sts for back, bind off 8(11,12) sts. Change to straight needles and work chart for Front, decreasing 1 st each side every other row 6 times. When armhole measures 7(7½, 7½) inches, work 22(24,27) sts. Place remaining 46(50,53) sts on holder. Dec 1 st neck edge every other row 6 times. Work till armhole measures 9(9½,10) inches. At armhole edge, bind off 5(6,7) sts twice, 6(6,7) sts once. Work other side to correspond, leaving center 20 sts on holder for neck ribbing.

Back and Neck

Work to correspond to front, but don't do neck. (Design on back is optional.) Sew shoulders, and using 16-inch smaller needle, pick up sts for neck ribbing. Work 5 rows main color in K2,P1 ribbing, 2 rows white. Bind off loosely, using larger needle.

Work ribbing at armhole to match neck if you are making a vest.

For Pullover
Sleeves

Using smaller needles and white, cast on 45(51,57) sts. Work K2,P1 ribbing for 2 rows, then change to main color. Work till ribbing measures 3 inches. Change to larger needles and work 2 rows of main color, the Pattern E twice. Then continue in main color. At the same time incr 1 st each end every 8th row 9(10,11) times. Work till sleeve measures 18(19,20)inches or desired length to underarm. *Sleeve Cap:* Bind off 4(5,6)sts beg next 2 rows, then dec 1 st each end every other row till 24 sts remain. Dec 1 st each end every row 4 times. Bind off remaining sts. Sew seams. Weave in ends. Block gently.

Men's Lobster Vest

Men's Lobster Pullover

(Pattern p. 61)

■ = Green.

☒ = White.

◿ = Teal.

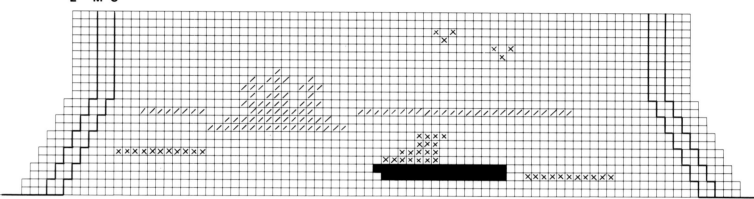

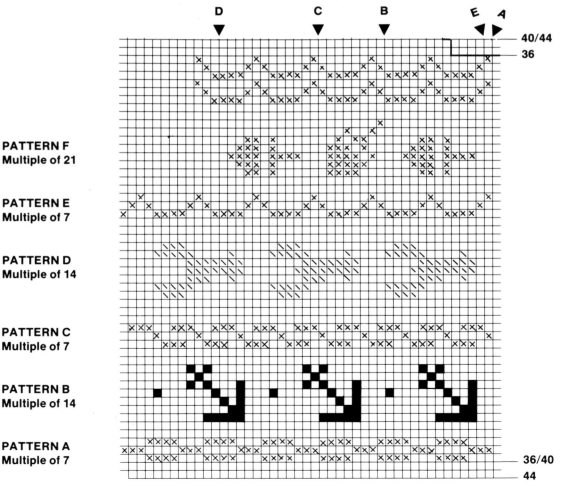

PATTERN F
Multiple of 21

PATTERN E
Multiple of 7

PATTERN D
Multiple of 14

PATTERN C
Multiple of 7

PATTERN B
Multiple of 14

PATTERN A
Multiple of 7

Versatile Cable Pullover

(Gauge 4½ sts = 1 inch)

This is the same pattern as our cable pullover but written for a stitch gauge of 4½ stitches per inch (instead of 4) making it perfect for many cottons and cotton/wool blend yarns. You can use it with any pattern designed to use the wool cable pattern.

Needles: US 5 and 8—or whatever size needed to get a stitch gauge of 4½ sts = 1 inch.
Sizes: 36,(38,40)
Materials: See Page 65

Front

With smaller needles, cast on 81(84,90) sts. Work K2,P1 ribbing for 3¼ inches, increasing 5(6,4) sts evenly in last row, 86(90,94). Change to larger needles and proceed as follows:

Row 1: K12(14,16),P2,K6,P2,K6,P2,K26, P2,K6,P2, K6,P2,K12(14,16).

Row 2: P12(14,16),K2,P6,K2,P6,K2,P26, K2,P6,K2,P6,K2,P12(14,16).

Rows 3,5: Same as Row 1.

Rows 4,6: Same as Row 2.

Row 7: K12(14,16),P2,C6b (do this cable by slipping 3 sts to holder, hold in back of work, K3,K3 from holder), P2,C6b,P2,K26, P2,C6f (slip 3 sts to holder, hold in front of work, K3,K3 from holder), P2,C6f,P2,K12 (14,16).

Rows 8,10,12,14: Same as Row 2.

Rows 9,11,13: Same as Row 1.

Row 15: Repeat Row 7.

Continue knitting the K sts and purling the P sts as established, with no more cabling until work measures 11½(12,12) inches. This is the measurement that will determine length of sweater. Finished sweater length is 14(14½, 14½) inches. *Any adjustments should be made now.* Repeat rows 7-15, then rows 2 and 3 once.

With wrong side facing you, *knit* the next 3 rows to make 2 ridges on the right side of work.

START CHART...

Armholes

Bind off 9 sts at beg of next 2 rows, 68(72,76) sts. Decrease first st on each of the next 10 rows by slipping 1 st, working the 2nd st, and passing the slipped st over it, 58(62,66) sts. Continue following chart, row for row, until neck opening is reached. On right side, work 20(22,24) sts, placing remaining sts on holder. Decrease 1 st every other row at neck edge 4 times, 16(18,20) sts. Bind off 5(6,7) sts at shoulder edge 2 times. Bind off remaining 6 sts. Leave center 18 sts on holder, and work other side to correspond.

Back

Work as for front for all shapings except neck. Do not follow charted design on back; rather, work stockinette sts above ridges. Work shoulders, leaving center 26 sts on holder.

Sleeves

With smaller needles, cast on 42(42,46) sts. Work K2,P1 ribbing for 3 inches, increasing 4(6,5) sts in last row, 46(48,50) sts. Change to larger needles, and establish sleeve cable as follows: Row 1, K14(15,16),P2,K6,P2, K6,P2,K14(15,16). Continue working the cable as for front, while increasing 1 st each side every 8th row 7 times, 60(62,64) sts. Work until sleeve measures 14½ inches. This measurement is for a 17-inch sleeve length. *Any adjustments should be made now.* Twist cables again (pattern rows 7-15). Work pattern Rows 2 and 3 once. With wrong side facing, knit next 3 rows.

Sleeve Cap

Bind off 9 sts at beg of next 2 rows. Decrease 1 st at beg of every row in same manner as for armhole, until 20 sts remain. Bind off 3 sts at beg of next 4 rows. Bind off remaining sts.

Finishing

Sew left shoulder-seam. Pick up approx 72 sts on smaller needles, and work in K2,P1 for 1 inch. Bind off loosely in ribbing using larger needles. Sew remaining seams; weave in all ends.

Seagull Pullover

Materials (Pattern p. 21):
Wool Knitting Worsted, 4 sts = in.
5 (4 oz.) skeins Main Color
1 (4 oz.) skeins Sky Color
30 yds White

Materials (Pattern p. 64):
Cotton or Cotton/Wool, 4½ sts = in.
1200 yds Main Color
200 yds Sky Color
30 yds White

Add 4 sts each side for gauge of 4½ sts = 1 inch. ▶

NECK RIBBING
● 2 rows darker green.
● 2 rows white.
● 2 rows darker green. Bind off loosely using larger needle.

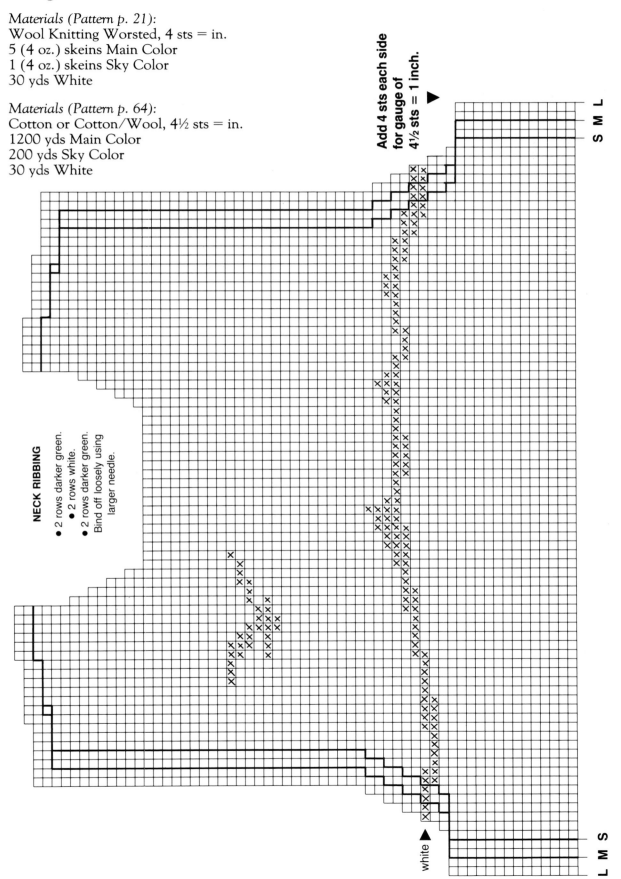

Seagull Pullover

Siamese Cats Cardigan

Siamese Cats Cardigan

Warren is my sleek Seal Point Siamese. He often reaches up to rattle the door knob, letting me know he wants to come in or out of a room and this is just what he is doing in this sweater. Knitting the sweater in a combination of purples suggests a Lavender Point Siamese.

Needle: Size 7—24″ circular needle—or whatever size needed to get a stitch gauge of 5 sts = 1 in.
Bobbins: 1 pack
Size: Medium
Materials:
5 (4 oz) skeins Main Color
1 (4 oz) skeins Natural White
1 (4 oz) skeins Contrasting Color

Size note

To make a larger size, add a stitch or two in between cats or knit on a size larger needle. Do the opposite for a size smaller.

Body

Cast on 182 sts on circular needle using bottom color of chart. When doing knit side, work chart right to left. Purl side goes left to right. Decide on length of sweater now so that buttonholes will be evenly spaced. The first buttonhole is worked at the end of the 6th row. [To make buttonhole: Purl to within 5 sts of end, bind off 5th and 4th stitches. Work to end. Next row, cast on 2 sts above bound-off stitches.] Cardigan length from underarm will be approx 13 inches if buttonholes are worked every 3⅜ inches, or approx 15 inches if worked every 3¾ inches. Work chart starting at right side working to the left, using bobbins so you don't have to carry colors. Work to armhole, ending on wrong side.

—CENTER FRONT

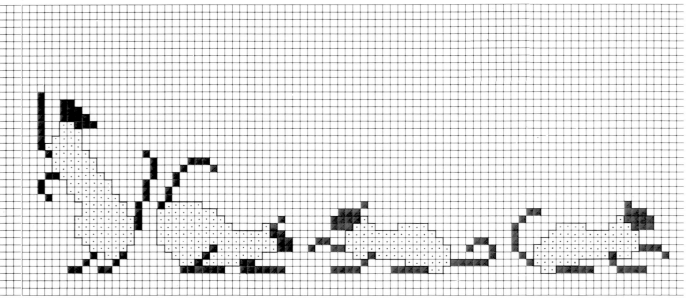

Armholes

Next row: Knit 42 sts, bind off next 10 sts for armhole. Work 78 sts for back, bind off 10 sts for armhole. Work 42 sts for other front. Purl next row, attaching balls of yarn where needed. Next row: dec 1 st each side of armhole this row, and again next 4 knit rows (5 times in all). Continue till armhole measures 5 inches (about 3 rows beyond last buttonhole), end on wrong side.

Neck

Bind off 12 sts beginning next two rows. Dec 1 st each side of neck every other row 4 times. Work till armhole is 7½ inches. Bind off 7 sts at each armhole edge next 6 rows. Then bind off 26 sts of back neck.

Sew shoulders from right side, matching stitch for stitch.

Sleeves

Cast on 44 sts. Work in stockinette stitch for 2 inches. Incr 1 st each side every 8th row 6 times (56 sts) till 16½ inches of desired length to underarm. Bind off 5 sts beginning next 2 rows. Dec 1 st each end every knit row till 20 sts remain. Bind off 2 sts beginning next 4 rows. Bind off remaining 12 sts.

Trim

Trim is worked in stockinette stitch. Cast on 6 sts of contrasting color. Work a long-enough strip to go around sweater's bottom, up fronts, and around neck. Also knit two strips for cuffs of sleeves. To attach, put right sides together and use a back stitch. Take a ¼″ tuck in trim for a nice sharp corner. Trim will curl around. Slip stitch on wrong side if you wish. Block pieces, sew seams right-side together using back stitch. Weave in ends. Sew on buttons.

■ = **same as trim color.**
⊡ = **natural white.**

—CENTER FRONT

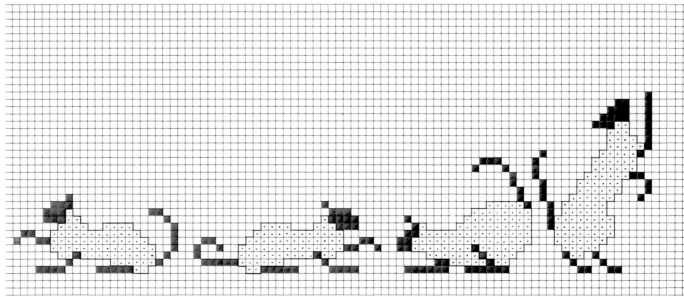

Teddy Bear Sweater

Teddy Bear Sweater

A Teddy Bear poking his head through a wreath on a sweater all tied up with ribbon—surely feels like Christmas! For more of a year round coloring we suggest a heather blue background with green and white ribbon. A favorite either way!

Needles: Sizes 5 and 9—or whatever size needed to get a stitch gauge of 4 sts = 1 inch.
Size: 36(38,40)
Materials:
5 (4 oz.) skeins Main Color
100 yds Center stripe of Ribbon
100 yds Dark Green
5 yds Med. Brown
2 yds Dark Brown
2 yds Light Brown

Front
With smaller needles, cast on 71(71,76) sts.
   Row 1: P1,K1B (knit in back of stitch), P1,K2. Repeat across row, ending P1.
   Row 2: K1*,P2,K1,P1,K1—repeat from * across row, ending K1.
   Row 3: P1,K1B,P1,K2 tog, then K first st again before removing from needle to form twist; repeat across row, ending P1.
   Row 4: same as row 2. Repeat these four rows for 3 inches. Increase 4(8,7) sts evenly across last row of ribbing: 75(79,83) sts. Change to larger needles and K17(19,21), work popcorn (K in front, back, front, back, front of same st, then slip 2nd, 3rd, 4th, and 5th sts over first one to form popcorn), K1, attach bobbin of Color A and K1, K1 MC, attach bobbin of Color B and K3, K1 MC, attach another bobbin of Color A and K1, K1 MC, work popcorn, K47(49,51). Row 2 and all even rows: purl across row, working colors as indicated. Row 3: knit across, working colors as indicated. Repeat these four rows until 12 popcorn rows have been completed. Here's where you decide on length of sweater. Direction are written for an underarm length of 13½ inches. If you want it longer, add 4 rows for every ¾ inch approx. *Now it's time to work the chart,* adding bobbins of colors as needed, binding off for armholes when it's time, and also to work neck and shoulders. *Armholes:* Bind off 5 sts beg next 2 rows. Decrease 1 st each end every knit row 5 times.

Neck
Work 19(21,23) sts, slip remaining sts on holder, decrease 1 st neck edge every other row 4 times. Bind off shoulder as indicated on chart. Work other side to correspond.

Back
Work same as front except follow Back chart for placement of colors. Work chart right up to shoulders. Place back neck stitches on holder.

Sleeves
Using smaller needles, cast on 38(38, 41) sts. Work ribbing same as front and back for 3 inches. Increase 3(5,4) sts evenly across last row of ribbing. Change to larger needles: work 15(16, 17) sts MC either side of ribbon of colors and popcorns (11 sts). Total: 41(43,45) sts. Increase 1 st each end every 8th row 7 times. When ready to work 17th popcorn row, follow chart and decrease for armhole. This will give a finished sleeve length of 16½ inches. *Armhole:* Bind off 5 sts beg next 2 rows. Decrease 1 st each end every other row till 21 sts remain. Decrease 1 st each end every row 4 times. Bind off remaining sts.

Neck Ribbing
Sew left shoulder seam. Using smaller needle, knit 25 back neck sts;pick up and knit 12 sts each side of neck plus 17 sts on holder. Work ribbing of K1,P1 for 10 rows. Next row increase 10 sts evenly across row. Change to ribbing as for front and back and cuffs, being careful that right side will be showing when neck is turned down. Work for 3 inches. Bind off loosely using larger needle. Sew seams. Weave in ends.

Adult Teddy Bear Sweater

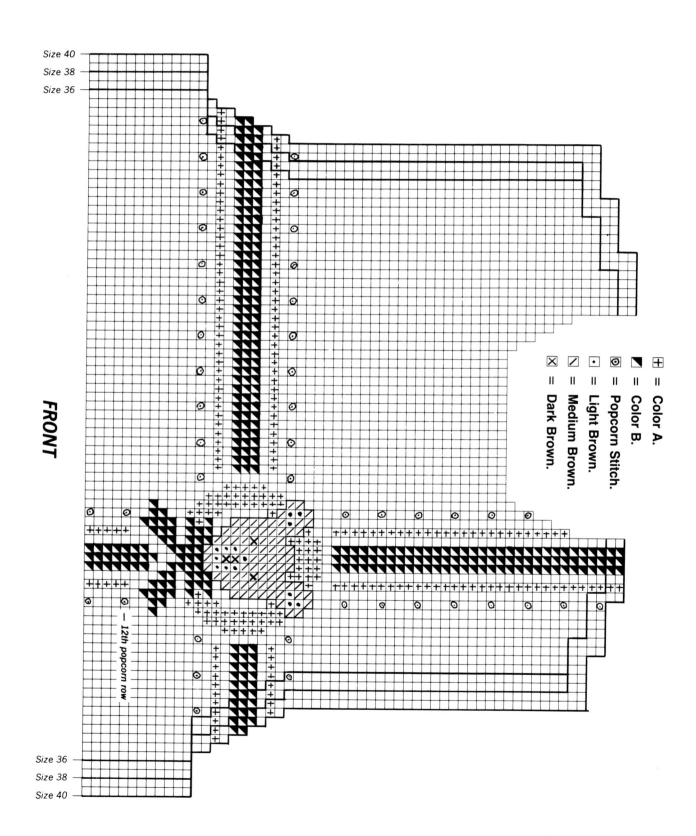

FRONT

Size 40
Size 38
Size 36

Size 36
Size 38
Size 40

— 12th popcorn row —

⊞ = Color A.
◣ = Color B.
◎ = Popcorn Stitch.
• = Light Brown.
∕ = Medium Brown.
☒ = Dark Brown.

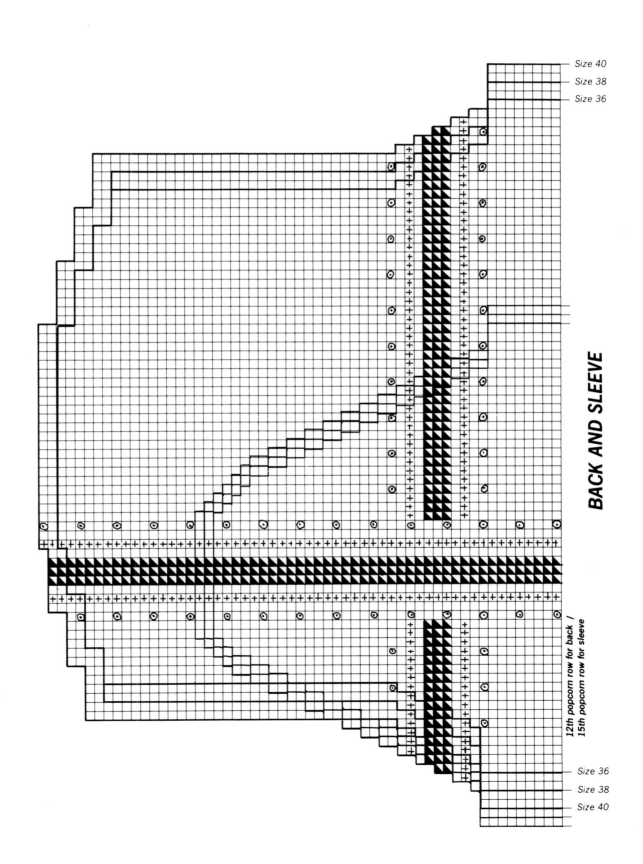

Size 40
Size 38
Size 36

BACK AND SLEEVE

12th popcorn row for back /
15th popcorn row for sleeve

Size 36
Size 38
Size 40

Chicken Sweater in Cotton

For those who love our chickens but don't want to knit with wool, here is the chicken pattern designed for 4½ stitches to the inch—perfect for cotton or cotton/wool blends. Use with the graph on page 13.

Needles: Size US 5 and 8—or whatever size needed to get gauge of 4½ sts = 1 in.
Sizes: 38 (40,42)
Materials:
1200 yds Main Color
20 yds each White & Peach for Chickens
5 yds each Plum and Yellow

Front

Using larger needle, cast on 81(87,90) sts. Change to smaller needles and work K2,P1 for 4 inches, increasing 6(4,5) sts evenly across in last row of ribbing. Change to larger needles and follow chart (p. 13) for front panel. Work till 13½(14,14) inches or desired length. End right side. With wrong side facing you, knit next 3 rows to form 2 ridges on right side of work. *Armholes:* Bind off 9 sts beg next 2 rows, also work design. Decrease 1 st each end every other row 5 times.

At neck, work 20(22,24) sts. Place remaining sts on holder. Decrease 1 st every other row at neck edge 4 times. Bind off 5(6,7) sts at shoulder edge 2 times, then 6(6,6) sts. Leave 19 center sts on holder. Work remaining 20 (22,24) sts to correspond.

Back

Cast on 81(87,90) sts. Work same as front until 13½(14,14) inches or desired length. Continue panel of "chicken wire" all the way up back, and do armholes same as front. Work shoulders and place 27 sts of neck on holder.

Sleeves

Cast on 42(46,46) sts. Rib in K2,P1 for 3 inches. Increase 5(4,6) sts last row of ribbing. Change to larger needles and follow chart for panel. Knit 10(11,12) sts, work 27 sts for panel, knit 10(11,12) sts. Increase 1 st each side every 8th row 7 times. Work on 61(63,65) sts until 17 inches or desired length to underarm. Bind off 9 sts beg next 2 rows. Decrease 1 st beg of every row, same as armhole, until 24 sts remain. Bind off 3 sts beg next 4 rows. Bind off remaining sts.

Finishing

Sew left shoulder seam. Pick up and knit sts on holders and 12(12,14) sts at each neck edge. Work ribbing of K2,P1 for 1 inch. Bind off very loosely using larger needles. Sew seams, and weave ends in.

Design Your Own

At the suggestion of Cris, part of our crew and an avid knitter, we decided to include two blank grids to give you the opportunity to do some designing of your own. Our favorite pullover, the versatile cable design, has a wonderful yoke that (as you can see through our various designs) lends itself to almost any pattern you can create. Using the two grids that follow and the compatible patterns we encourage you to design your own sweater.

First, we suggest, be brave and don't think twice about your ability to do this. We all have some designs tucked away in us somewhere and this is your chance to bring them out. If you can't think of anything, look in a favorite cross stitch pattern book—those patterns are very adaptable and they are already charted for you.

Begin by taking these pages of blank grids to a photocopier and making several copies. This will give you lots of opportunities to try different ideas and perfect them. As you work on them—think about your hobbies or a favorite animal. Are you a wildflower or exotic bird fancier? Does your grandchild have a special stuffed animal or your son or daughter a favorite sport?

Once you have chosen your design, here are a few suggestions about working with motif type designs that we have learned over the years:
• Keep the design in from the edges—you don't want to lose a critical element to the curve in a person's body.
• The major theme should be off center for the best look.
• Odd numbers of objects are usually better. (We broke this rule with the chicken sweater.)
• When you are using several different colors of yarn, leave the texture stitches to a minimum and when using lots of texture, keep the number of colors to a minimum.
• Give designing a try—remember you can always rip it out and replace it with one of the designs we have provided.

Pullover Grid

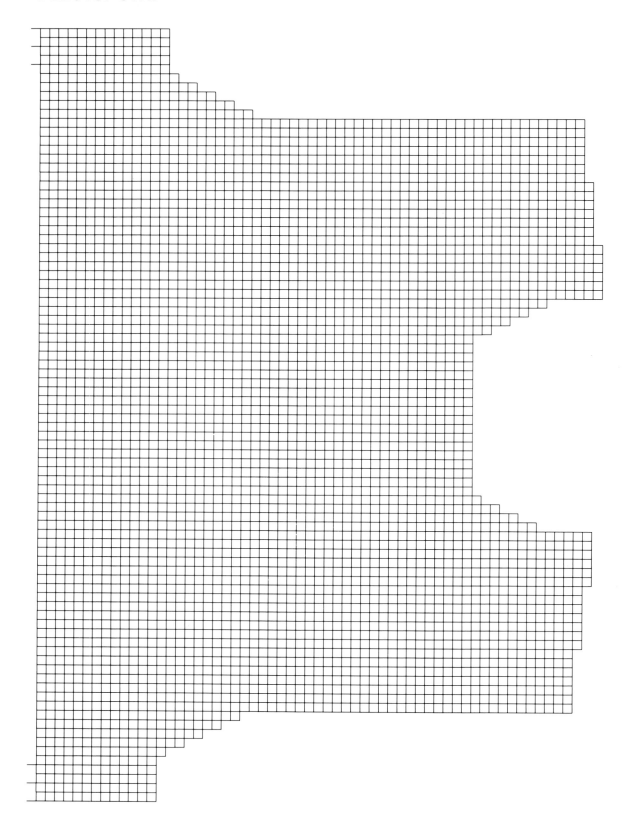

Cardigan Grid

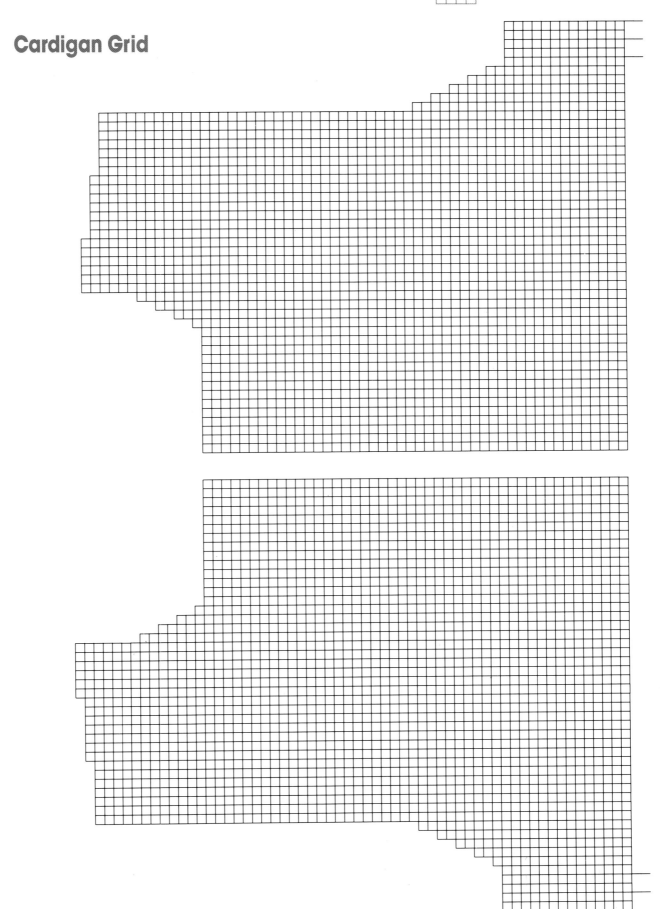

The Bartlett Mill

Our association with Bartlettyarns goes back to the years when I first had sheep. We have enjoyed doing business with this small, friendly company where the president often answers the phone. Many of our designs have been inspired by the beautiful heather colors in their fisherman and tweed yarns.

Located in the town of Harmony, in the central farming and forestry region of Maine, the mill began operation in 1821. It remained in the Bartlett family until the 1940's and since 1981 has been owned by Russ Pierce.

When the mill was started, the production of woven fabric was an important source of supplemental income in northern New England. Most homes had a loom and sometimes several women would work together in one home. The cloth was sold to merchants in Boston, suggesting to Russ Pierce that northern New England was perhaps in those days the equivalent of New York City's garment district today.

The business thrived on the demand for the home loomed fabric and often took wool in trade for yarn from the farmers who raised sheep. The mill was sited on Higgins Stream and had an earthen dam and water wheel. With water for about half a year's production—spinning would start early in the spring after shearing and continue until the heat of summer when the stream dried up. With fall rains, spinning could begin again.

The mill operates now with a workforce very similar to the earlier days—two dozen employees. Having survived one fire, today's building (from the 1920's) has about twice the floor space of the original and the output of spun yarn is about double because electricity is used rather than waterpower. What hasn't changed is the quality of the yarn produced by the mule spinning process, a procedure which only Bartlettyarns (in this country) has kept commercially alive.

The mule spinner uses a 200 year old technique from England which was once common in this country. It is called "mule" because it mimics an old fashioned hand spinning process done with a walking wheel. The mule technique is coupled with the "woolen system," a term used to describe the combing of the fibers that produces a homespun type yarn for spinning that has short fibers and a soft fuzzy texture.

There are several steps in the long process of producing yarn from sheep's wool. Shearing is the first step and usually takes place in early spring before the sheep are put out to pasture. Bartlettyarns buys the fleece and must first have it scoured. The technique used involves five or six washings to remove the excess lanolin, dirt and chaff (vegetable matter—hay and burrs, etc.). A delicate balance must be maintained to make the yarn of high quality yet retain enough lanolin to keep its soft and weather resistant qualities.

The fleece is then dyed in a commercial dyehouse and returned to Harmony where it is blended with undyed fleece creating its heather effect. The next step in the process is called "picking" (or "teasing," as it was once done with a teasel weed) which opens up and fluffs the wool. It is then "dusted"— in a machine employing centrifugal force to rid it of the remaining foreign matter.

The purpose of the next step, "carding," is to discipline the fibers into long parallel strands to produce "rovings"—fat strands of untwisted yarn. Finally, the yarn is spun on the mule spinner and wound onto a bobbin. The "twisting" procedure then takes this single plied yarn and plies it into the double ply yarn that is then skeined and sent to consumers such as us.

Bartlettyarns sells these yarns both wholesale and retail. Check with them to see if there is a dealer in your area, and if not, ask for a sample card. Then, the next time you knit a sweater using those wonderful mule spun yarns—you can think about their long journey from the sheep into your sweater!!

Sources of Supplies

As you can see from our earlier suggestions, we have a clear bias for natural materials—wool, cotton and cotton wool blends. You may also want to try knitting one of these sweaters in more exotic yarns—raw silk, alpaca, angora, whatever your imagination dictates.

When looking for your materials, we suggest you search out your local yarn shop, and avoid your local discount department store. The yarn shop owner will likely be a knowledgeable knitter who can help you in making yarn decisions and will be there when you run into difficult times. Such shops will likely have many wonderful yarns for you to choose from. They are most likely also struggling small businesses in need of your support—you'll never know how much you depended on them until they are gone.

If you can't find what you need, all of the materials shown in this book can be ordered directly from us or any of the sources listed below. We sell both kits and skeined yarns and buttons. Contact us at the following address for brochures, prices and ordering information:

North Island Designs, Inc
Main Street
North Haven, Maine 04853
1-800-548-5648 or 207-867-2004

Other Suppliers Include:
For 100% Wool, Fisherman Type Yarns
Bartlettyarns, Inc.
Harmony, ME 04942
207-683-2251
They sell directly through the mail
or can let you know the nearest
retailer carrying their product.

Briggs & Little Woolen Mills, Ltd.
Harvey Station
York Mills, NB Canada EOH 1HO
506-366-5438
Sell direct as well as through
retailers in this country.

Green Mountain Spinnery
P.O. Box 568
Putney, VT 05346
800-321-WOOL

For Wool and Wool/Cotton Blends
Brown Sheep Co.
Route 1
Mitchell, Nebraska 69357
800-826-9136
They can tell you your nearest dealer.

Pewter Buttons
Norwegian Pewter Buttons
Available through us.

Maiden Vermont Buttons
Danforth Pewters
RD1, Box 292
Bristol, Vermont 05443
802-453-3191

Ceramic Buttons—a wonderful way to liven up a cardigan! (See the Whimsical chicken vest)
Hands Work
P.O. Box 386
Pecos, New Mexico
505-757-6730
They will let you know of a dealer near you.

Penny Straker
P.O. Box 211
South Dartmouth, Massachusetts 02748
617-996-4804
Call for dealer name.

Wooden Needles Our favorite to knit with!
Merrills of Maine
P.O. Box 1619
Wolfeboro, NH 03894
603-569-2467

NORTH ISLAND DESIGNS

INCORPORATED

ou may contact us directly if
ou are unable to find any of the
aterials we have recommended
 the book. We have kits, yarn
cks (a kit without the pattern)
d skeined yarns. We are also
re to answer your knitting
estions and you can reach us
rough our toll free number.

 If you would like our color
ochure or yarn sample cards
7 ppd) just call or send us one
 these postpaid cards. Once
ur name is on our mailing list,
u will receive our quarterly
ewsletter with descriptions of
r latest designs as well as news
om the island.

all our toll free number:
-800-548-5648
r in Maine:
-867-4788
r send in one of the
tached cards.

Please Send Me . . . *Your Catalog and Price List.*

Name_____

Street Address_____

Town_____ State_____ Zip_____

. . . Add a friend to your mailing list!

Name_____

Street Address_____

Town_____ State_____ Zip_____

Phone Orders: 1-800-548-5648 In Maine 1-867-4788

CB

. . . Here are some friends *for your mailing list!*

Name_____

Street Address_____

Town_____ State_____ Zip_____

Name_____

Street Address_____

Town_____ State_____ Zip_____

CB

o **Order Books**:

end in the card opposite to
der any of our titles.
 Since this card goes to a
fferent address, be sure to send
 one of the top cards to place
ur name on *our* mailing list.
 To receive a free Down East
talog of fine books and gifts,
ll 207-594-9544
 1-800-766-1670.

Down East Books
P.O. Box 679, Camden, Maine 04843

ORDER FORM

Quantity	Item	Price	Total
	1 — Maine Island Classics	$15.95	
	2 — Maine Island Kids	$15.95	
	3 — Sweaters from the Maine Islands	$16.95	
	4 — North Island Designs 4	$17.95	

METHOD OF PAYMENT

Mastercard_____ Visa_____ Check_____

Acct. #_____ Exp. Date_____

Signature_____

Name_____

Address_____

_____ Tel._____

Subtotal	
Me. Res. 6% Sales Tax	
Shipping*	
TOTAL	

*Add $3.25 for first book, $1.00
for each additional book. We ship
UPS unless you specify otherwise.

BUSINESS REPLY MAIL

FIRST CLASS   PERMIT NO. 1   NORTH HAVEN, MAINE

POSTAGE WILL BE PAID BY ADDRESSEE

North Island Designs
Main Street
North Haven, ME
04853

BUSINESS REPLY MAIL

FIRST CLASS   PERMIT NO. 1   NORTH HAVEN, MAINE

POSTAGE WILL BE PAID BY ADDRESSEE

North Island Designs
Main Street
North Haven, ME
04853

PLEASE ENCLOSE THIS ORDER FORM
(WITH PAYMENT, IF PAYING BY CHECK)
IN AN ENVELOPE AND
RETURN TO:

Down East Books

P.O. Box 679, Camden, Maine 04843